APPRENTICING STUDENTS INTO SCIENCE

DOING, TALKING & WRITING SCIENTIFICALLY

Published by Lexis Education
Melbourne, Australia
www.lexised.com

National Library of Australia Cataloguing-in-Publication entry

Creator:	Polias, John, author.
Title:	Apprenticing students into science : doing, talking & writing scientifically / John Polias.
ISBN:	9780646952604 (paperback)
Notes:	Includes bibliographical references and index.
Subjects:	Science--Study and teaching.
	Science teachers--Training of.
Dewey No:	507.1

Layout, design and all unattributed photographs by Carl Nilsson-Polias

Contents

Introduction	6
Generic activities in school science	10
Sample texts in school science	17
Macrogenres	51
Multiple ways of making meaning	57
Consolidating scientific behaviour	63
A model of language for educators	69
Scaffolding in the science classroom	77
Cycles of teaching and learning	101
Language resources for 'doing' science	107

Acknowledgements

I would like to express my gratitude to the hundreds of science teachers in Hong Kong and Australia who have undertaken the science courses that have given rise to this book.

I would especially like to thank the following teachers, whose work can be seen in the many classroom examples in the book:

Hong Kong
LEE Sze Man
LEUNG Man Fai Mario
LEUNG Wing Cheuk Terence
LING Chi Yeung
NGAN Shiu Hei
TSANG Wai Cheung Zinc
WONG Sui Bun
YUNG Chi Hang Felix

Australia
Gail HAMILTON
Anna PETROCCHI

John Polias is an international consultant in teaching and learning with a focus on language, especially in multilingual learning contexts. He is a science, mathematics, visual arts and linguistics graduate. Much of his work has been in partnership with the South Australian Department of Education and Child Development, The Education Bureau of Hong Kong, and The Hong Kong Polytechnic University. As one of the two directors of Lexis Education, he writes and delivers professional development courses for international schools around the world. His interests lie in developing cross-curriculum pedagogies that are underpinned by the role of language but which also have a multisemiotic approach.

Introduction

This is a book for teachers of science who wish to maximise the learning in their classrooms by basing their teaching according to a number of factors:

- using the identifiable patterns in scientific knowledge and making those patterns explicit to the students
- understanding and applying the patterns of language that construe science
- understanding the potential of non-language meaning-making resources
- applying an understanding of linguistic and non-linguistic patterns so that students are provided multiple access points to the meanings
- using a teaching and learning cycle that is based on highly applicable theories of language and thought
- recycling the meanings within the teaching and learning cycle by understanding better the kinds of interactions that scaffold students in science classrooms.

This book's aim is to show how the patterns in school science allow it to do what it does. Through this kind of understanding of science will come better science teaching. This is not as matter-of-fact as it might first appear. Many science teachers have become so immersed in their field that they have lost sight of what it is like to be a student of science. In other words, the ways that scientific concepts are construed of meanings has become implicit and teachers find it difficult to make explicit the implicit. This book's ambition is to rectify this situation — denaturalising the naturalised science knowledge — because an awareness of that can help teachers know what it is that needs to be done and how it needs to be done most effectively and efficiently so learning is maximised.

In addition, by examining how meanings are made in science, teachers are able to argue for why and how they do what they do. So, instead of using nebulous terms such as a science activity engendering interest in students or an activity being fun, teachers should be able to explain why an activity promotes curiosity and maintains interest. In the most basic of terms, motivation and interest are sustained through achieving success in learning and that would require implementing a pedagogy that provides students with continued success within a lesson and across many lessons. In other words, a pedagogy that scaffolds students into a deeper understanding of the scientific knowledge creates the critical engagement that we wish to promote in students.

Ways we mean in science

The work of Jay Lemke, for example, stresses that science is multimodal or multisemiotic ('multi-meaning'):

> "Science is not done, is not communicated, through verbal language alone. It cannot be. The 'concepts' of science are not solely verbal concepts, though they have verbal components. They are semiotic hybrids, simultaneously and essentially verbal, mathematical, visual-graphical, and actional-operational. ... To do science, to talk science, to read and write science it is necessary to juggle and combine in various canonical ways verbal discourse, mathematical expression, graphical-visual representation, and motor operations in the world."
> (Lemke 1998: 87)

Taking a multisemiotic approach to teaching and learning has the potential for providing the student multiple access points to the knowledge being taught. In this way, the patterns in the scientific knowledge become 'visible' and 'audible' to the students so they are not left having to work with opaque meanings or guessing. However, providing multiple access points to the meanings is not sufficient if the method of teaching does not match the patterns in the knowledge itself. The method of teaching has to match these patterns so that both the semiotic resources and the teaching methodology work in harmony. I have named this pedagogical resonance, borrowing the resonance notion from physics, where waves cancel or reinforce each other.

> "So the metaphor is that, when the 'how-we-teach wave' and the 'what-we-want-to-teach wave' are synchronised so that they resonate with each other, we achieve heightened learning."
> (Polias 2010)

A teaching and learning cycle

Apart from the patterns of meanings in scientific knowledge, we will also consider a patterned teaching and learning cycle that is informed by Vygotskian thinking (Vygotsky 1963) and the concept of scaffolding (Wood, Bruner & Ross 1976). Scaffolding will be considered at the levels of macro-, meso- and micro-scaffolding. We will see that the teaching and learning cycle can be constructed as a complex circling and spiralling of these three levels of scaffolding.

Language — a resource for making meaning

Language, as our primary resource for making meaning (Halliday 1975), provides the means for developing and accessing abstract and technical meanings. We can take the example of small children constructing a technical classification through language alone. In the following text (Painter 1996: 64), a young child, four-year-old Stephen (S), cannot find a picture of a seal in his book about fish so his older brother Hal (H) helps him out:

H: Seals aren't fish. That's why. They're mammals.
S: Are seals mammals?
H: Yes, 'cause they don't lay eggs; they have babies.

The class of mammals is constructed through language; there is nothing concrete about the taxonomy. So Stephen has developed this knowledge (that one can classify animals in technical ways) through a schooled child, his six-year-old brother Hal. It was Stephen's linguistic ability that enabled him to understand the criterion that was presented by his brother linguistically. Another example from Painter's research (1996: 65) is the following in which Stephen (S) and his mother (M) are discussing whether whales kill people:

M: There may be one kind of whale that can, but most whales are nice creatures
S: They're not creatures Mum, they're whales
M: Yes; creatures is anything that's alive
S: Are we creatures?
M: Yeh
S: No, we're not! (laughing).

Painter (1996: 67) states further that, as the child's ability to use language expands, it opens up new possibilities for thinking and learning.

The model of language that allows us to understand language as a resource for making meaning is the Hallidayan systemic-functional model of language (Halliday & Hasan 1985, Halliday & Matthiessen 2014). This approach to language will be complemented in this book by the research on genre for educational purposes (Martin 2012). Halliday's systemic-functional model is an appliable linguistic model and is applied in this book in talking about the patterns of language in science. Any discussion of specific language patterns in this book are pertinent to the English language.

Generic activities in school science

Science is a highly complex sociocultural construct. It is cultural in the sense that there is a large community of people who can recognise themselves as belonging to a group of professionals called scientists because their approaches to the physical world are recognisable and predictable to each other. Science is social in the sense that the body of knowledge that might be seen as constituting science is co-constructed by members of this cultural group. Through this co-construction — where scientists agree and disagree, polemicise and problematise — science undergoes change.

These patterned sociocultural activities that are recognisable and predictable by a cultural group are generic activities; that is, activities that are generalisable. These are known as genres (e.g. Martin & Rose 2008, Hedeboe & Polias 2008). Science could then be seen as consisting of a set of genres and, by enacting these genres, the cultural group called scientists comes into being. The genres both identify the members of the group and are identified by the same members. To summarise, we can say the following:

- Science, as a sociocultural construct, comes into being by being enacted through generic activities and evolves as scientists communicate with other scientists.
- Scientists set out with a purpose in mind, such as how to test something through experimentation, how to explain

a physical phenomenon, and how to construct a technical taxonomy, and these purposes are enacted through generic activities.

- The generic activities unfold in patterned ways, giving them predictable structures, predictable visuals and predictable language patterns.

Educational genres as dynamic processes

If genre, as a sociocultural activity, is to be useful in educational contexts, where the students are being apprenticed into the various, valued educational genres, then it cannot be seen as simply the final representation on the page. It needs to be seen as a much more dynamic phenomenon, as a series of teaching and learning events that are directed towards configuring the meanings in the way they look on the page because there is an objective in mind with the activities.

Therefore, when teachers begin to plan, say, a test of what kind of gas is formed in a certain reaction, they know that, in the end, the documentation of that work will be a Laboratory Report. But, in their planning of the lesson(s), they need to be mindful of the fact that everything they do in the activities that lead up to that Laboratory Report is scaffolding the learning that is finally put down on paper. In other words, the Laboratory Report does not exist without all the activities — the thinking, doing, observing, talking, and noting — that make it exist. If teachers have this kind of understanding, they and their students would more easily understand that what is seen on the page and heard in discussions are a continuing, dynamic construction of the scientific knowledge.

Figure 1 sets out the genres that typically constitute school science (cf Veel 1997, Christie & Derewianka 2008). It is organised according to the major semiotic processes that make up science in schooling contexts — doing, describing and organising, explaining, and arguing, with acknowledging as a minor process. There is a tendency in the table's organisation to go from concrete, grounded meanings in the 'doing' genres to the more reflective and abstract meanings in the 'arguing' genres, and then within each set to start from the first mentioned in the set. This, as we will see, can provide teachers a macro-scaffold in designing a series of lessons within a unit of work. The second column has the genres listed — these are labels for the scientific processes.

Scientific processes	Genres	Purposes
doing things scientifically	Experiments and Protocols	To instruct someone in what to do to achieve a certain outcome
	Laboratory Reports	To provide a recount of the method taken, as well as the results, discussion and conclusions
	Investigations	To set out the design and decisions behind students' attempts to behave scientifically
describing and organising	Descriptions	To describe multiple aspects/features of a natural or physical phenomenon
	Comparisons	To compare features of two or more natural or physical phenomena
	Components	To present (describe and/or define) component parts of a natural or physical phenomenon
	Classifications	To present different types (classes) of a natural or physical phenomenon
explaining phenomena	*temporal* Sequential Explanations	To explain a natural or physical phenomenon by linking causally the chain of events producing the phenomenon
	non-temporal Factorial/Consequential Explanations	To explain the multiple factors or consequences that contribute to or are a result of a particular phenomenon
	non-temporal Theoretical Explanations	To define a theoretical principle and provide examples of its applications
arguing	Arguments	To persuade to agree with a particular point of view on an issue — two sub-types: agree-with-me arguments and agree-with-me-and-take-some-action arguments
	Discussions	To present the case for more than one point of view
acknowledging scientists	Biographies	To recount the major events in a famous scientist's life

Figure 1: The genres constituting school science

There are alternative taxonomics of the science genres: some have minor differences in the naming and the genres included (Martin & Rose 2008, Unsworth 2001, Christie & Derewianka 2008), while Matthiessen's taxonomy (2012) approaches generic activities as socio-semiotic processes.

In the next section, sample final texts of these generic activities are analysed and the patterns in their structural and linguistic features are discussed. This book uses an initial capital letter to identify a genre.

What do science curricula say about genre?

How explicit are curriculum documents about the generic activities that science teachers engage in with their students? Let us take three examples.

The Hong Kong Education Bureau's Integrated Science Curriculum & Assessment Guide (Secondary 4-6) (EDB 2009) states that for their core unit on Water for Living, students should learn about, for example:

- *The properties of water*
- *The movement of water in and out of cells by osmosis*
- *The water cycle*
- *The greenhouse effect*
- *The causes and effects of water problems (drought, desertification, soil erosion, flooding) in China.*

The Australian Curriculum (accessed Jan 2015 from http://www.australiancurriculum.edu.au) states that for 13-year-old students studying biological sciences, they will be learning about cells by engaging in the following activities.

Cells are the basic units of living things and have specialised structures and functions:

- *examining a variety of cells using a light microscope, by digital technology or by viewing a simulation*
- *distinguishing plant cells from animal or fungal cells*
- *identifying structures within cells and describing their function*
- *recognising that some organisms consist of a single cell*
- *recognising that cells reproduce via cell division*
- *describing mitosis as cell division for growth and repair.*

The Swedish science curriculum (accessed and translated by the author Oct 2014 from http://www.skolverket.se/laroplaner-amnen-och-kurser/grundskoleutbildning/grundskola/biologi) for students aged 13-15 states specifically for cells:

- *The body's cells, organs and body systems and their components, their functions and interdependence. Comparisons in terms of evolution of humans and other organisms.*

For its domain called 'Biological methods and ways of working', it states:

- *Field studies and experiments with the posing of simple questions to be investigated, planned, undertaken and evaluated.*
- *How organisms are identified and classified according to how they are related to other organisms and development.*
- *How different biological investigations are linked and the development of concepts, models and theories.*
- *Documentation of experiments and investigations with tables, diagrams, images and written reports.*
- *Critical analysis of sources of information and arguments with some connection to biology that students encounter in the discussions that occur in the wider community.*

The Swedish curriculum and Australian curriculum both have processes included in their description, making it easier to identify the generic processes: experimenting, investigating, classifying, explaining, comparing, researching past and present thinking, and appraising.

Hong Kong's document is more opaque in terms of processes but it is also possible to identify them: the properties of water is about describing and organising; movement of water in and out, the water cycle and greenhouse effect suggest explanations although all three may be made up of multiple genres (macrogeneric); and the causes and effects of water problems suggest explanations that are not sequenced in real-time. The latter would move into arguing if it stated something such as 'The causes and effects of water problems and the extent to which the Three Gorges Dam has intensified these problems along the Yangtze.'

So, sets of genres within curriculum descriptions can be identified even though some make the task of identifying them harder. Making explicit the generic demands of the science curriculum is part of the denaturalisation process for science teachers.

2

Sample texts in school science

In this section, sample texts of each of the science genres given in Figure 1 are examined and, for each one, a number of questions are asked in order to identify and discuss their generic characteristics, such as:

- What are the major features of the texts?
  - the overall purpose of the text (what it sets out to do or achieve or why it is being enacted)
  - the structural patterns of the text (the stages or the phases that the text goes through)
  - the major language patterns of the text
- Which genres are they examples of (which genres are being enacted)?

Further questions are centred around which of the texts are recognisable to teachers (and, ultimately, to students) and whether they can identify the kinds of tasks which require these kinds of texts.

Doing things scientifically

Experiment

Text 1

Aim

To test for starch in a green leaf.

Materials and apparatus

1 small green leaf
iodine solution
large test tube
water
ethanol
Bunsen burner
tripod
gauze mat
2 large beakers (250 cc)
forceps
glass rod
Petri dish
white tile
goggles

Method

1. Take a small green leaf from a healthy plant.
2. Boil some water in a beaker and then turn down the Bunsen flame.
3. Use forceps to dip the leaf into the boiling water for about one minute.
4. Take out the leaf and place it at the bottom of a large test tube—push it to the bottom with a glass rod.
5. Put on your goggles and then pour enough ethanol to cover the leaf.
6. Place the test tube with the leaf in the beaker of boiling water until all the chlorophyll (green colour) has dissolved out of the leaf.
7. Pour the alcohol, which is now green, into a spare beaker.
8. Using the forceps, remove the leaf from the test tube and dip it once in the boiling water to soften it.
9. Place the leaf flat in a Petri dish on a white tile.
10. Drop iodine solution so that it covers the entire leaf.
11. Observe any colour changes that occur.

Patterns in the structure

The generic structure of Experiments is essentially the following:

- The purpose of the activity — the aim or objective.
- The things needed for the activity — the materials and apparatus.
- The steps or individual actions to be done — the method or procedure.

Optional stages are: hypothesis, introduction and precautions.

If there are precautions, then they are typically included within the text, either as a separate step, 'Put on your goggles', or as the manner of the action, 'Carefully place 2 drops of sulphuric acid…' so that the action is successful.

A Protocol (e.g. 'How to behave in the laboratory') differs from an Experiment in that it does not need a separate stage to name any apparatus or materials. If any materials are needed, they are included in the steps (e.g. '…goggles, gloves…'), and there is no testing or the making of a product.

Patterns in the language

Experiments are written by someone who knows how to achieve the aims successfully and safely. There is usually an absence of negotiability and this means that the instructions are given in the most direct, least ambiguous way possible: the focus is on the action itself rather than the scientist.

When something in the context demands a shift in the orientation from the action, we can have other choices coming at the front, e.g. 'Using the forceps, remove the leaf…'. In this example, the reason for its use is both because of the need for safety and the difficulty of doing it without forceps.

The aim or objective of the Experiment is usually given in the form 'To test for starch…' but can sometimes be expressed in the form 'A test for starch…'.

Laboratory Report

Text 2

Title

Anaerobic respiration

Objective

To study the effect of different respiratory substrates (e.g. glucose, sucrose, starch) on the rate of respiration of yeast cells.

Background

Many yeasts of the genus Saccharomyces are facultative anaerobes. In the absence of oxygen, yeasts convert carbohydrate substrate into ethanol and carbon dioxide. The rate at which carbon dioxide is produced can be used as a measure of the overall rate of anaerobic respiration.

Apparatus and reagents

1 ml pipette
10 ml pipette
rubber tubing
water bath
boiling tube
thermometer
data logger (aMixer)
gas pressure sensor
5% yeast suspension
1% starch solution
1% glucose solution
0.1% glucose solution
1% sucrose solution
distilled water

Precaution

Use boiled water to prepare all the solutions to ensure minimum oxygen content.

Procedure

1. Label the five boiling tubes A, B, C, D and E, respectively.
2. Fill the labelled boiling tubes with 30 ml of 1% starch solution, 1% glucose solution, 0.1% glucose solution 1% sucrose solution and distilled water, respectively.
3. Add 15 ml of the activated yeast suspension to each boiling tube and shake the tube to ensure the yeast suspension and solution are mixed thoroughly.
4. Prepare a water bath of 34°C, place tube A into the bath and let it stand for 10 minutes to reach equilibrium.
5. Use a stopper to seal tube A and connect the stopper with rubber tubing to the gas pressure sensor and data logger.
6. Turn on the data logger and log the data for 5 minutes.
7. Collect data that show the rate of pressure change due to anaerobic respiration.
8. Repeat Steps 4 to 7 with tubes B, C, D and E, respectively. Tabulate all the results.

Results

Tube	*Respiratory substrate*	*Rate of pressure change/ kPas⁻¹*
A	1% starch solution	0.00213
B	1% glucose solution	0.03724
C	0.1% glucose solution	0.00679
D	1% sucrose solution	0.04569
E	distilled water	0.00312

Analysis and discussion

In an air tight environment, yeast cells will carry out anaerobic respiration and give out carbon dioxide.

Pyruvic acid –> ethanol + carbon dioxide

Since carbon dioxide is released as a by-product of anaerobic respiration, the volume of carbon dioxide gas inside the tube will increase, thus increasing the gas pressure inside the tube. The greater the increase in gas pressure, the faster the rate of respiration of yeast cells.

The results show that tube D (with 1% sucrose solution as substrate) has the fastest rate of respiration. It is because, with the aid of an enzyme, one sucrose molecule will be broken down into one fructose and one glucose molecule. As a result, tube D provides more respiratory substrates for yeast cells. The more respiratory substrates there are, the greater the rate of respiration. So tube D gives the highest respiratory rate.

For tube B, although it has the same concentration of substrate solutions as tube D, it shows a slower rate of respiration than that of tube D. This is probable because tube D contains both glucose and fructose, while tube B only contains glucose, so it has fewer substrates than tube D.

For tube A, since starch is a polysaccharide and the yeast may not have a relative enzyme to break it down, it shows a very slow respiratory rate. The small increase in pressure is mainly because yeast cells use their food store to carry out anaerobic respiration.

For tube C, since it contains very dilute glucose solution compared with tube B, it shows a very slow respiratory rate because fewer substrates mean a slower rate of respiration.

Tube E acts as a control for the experiment. However, even in the absence of respiratory substrate, tube E still shows a slow respiratory rate because the yeast cells use their food store to carry out anaerobic respiration.

It is possible that the rate of pressure change is not accurate because the yeast suspension in each boiling tube may not be evenly distributed.

Conclusion

Different respiratory substrates have different effects on the rate of respiration of yeast cells. It appears that the 1% sucrose solution shows the greatest rate of respiration of yeast cells, while the 1% starch solution shows the slowest. The respiratory rate of the 1% starch solution is approximately the same as that of distilled water.

■ 16-year-old student text (Polias 2005)

Investigation

Text 3

Introduction

In this experiment, we were asked to identify what might affect the growth of a plant. I chose to grow broccoli. We were to apply a variable to one of the plants and the other we were to use as a control. My variable was that the plant would grow better if I spoke Swedish to it.

Prediction

My prediction was that, if I spoke Swedish for 30 seconds to one plant (Veg 1) every time I went up to the plants, then it would grow better than the other.

The experiment

I used two small seedlings planted in two separate plastic pots filled with potting soil, and these were placed in the direct sunlight of the greenhouse. I put labelled sticks into the soil to identify the two plants: Veg 1 was the plant to be spoken to in Swedish, Veg 2 was the control.

The measuring of the plants and the recording of the data were pivotal to the experiment. I measured the weight (g) using spring scales, and the height and width (cm) using a ruler. This was done every time I went up to observe and water the plants. As part of my experiment, I also spoke for 30 seconds to Veg 1 every time. Both plants were treated exactly the same — that is, I made sure I gave the same amount of water, soil and sunlight to both plants — except, I spoke to Veg 1 in Swedish.

Results

The results across all three measurements were roughly the same towards the end while, in the early stages, the growth was quite erratic. Both were root bound when I removed them from their pots and this may explain the decrease in size and their weight loss. Veg 1 grew a head and flowered before Veg 2, and Veg 1's head was also bigger.

Conclusion

While speaking Swedish to my plant did not make much of a difference in growth, the plant that I spoke to did appear healthier but I can't say that my prediction was accurate without further tests.

I felt my measuring was relatively accurate. However, the time constraints imposed meant that error due to rushing was possible.

Perhaps ensuring that the amount of Swedish spoken was exactly the same each time could also help.

If I was to do the experiment again, I would like to be able to go and see the plants more often and grow more than two to improve the credibility of the results.

■ 14-year-old student text

Patterns in the structure

The generic structures of the Laboratory Report and Investigation are similar, but the student has designed the Investigation. So, whereas Laboratory Reports have an aim or objective, Investigations typically have a prediction. Both have what is titled an introduction or background. Although the background/introduction for the Laboratory Report is optional, it would appear to be a compulsory stage in the Investigation since the student needs to make explicit to the reader the context for the Investigation, which may not be so obvious in the prediction alone.

Also, Investigations may not list the materials to be used but instead have them as part of the method. That might be acceptable if the focus is not on someone else repeating the experiment but, as we see in the conclusion, the student suggests repeating the experiment so perhaps knowing exactly what materials were used as well as how they were used would help the reliability of a test.

The remaining parts of Investigations and Laboratory Reports unfold in similar ways: the method to be taken, the results and then a discussion of the results. The conclusion stage, though, might have different phases within it. As we can see in the Investigation, there is discussion about ways to improve its design. In a longer Investigation and at a higher level of complexity, we could expect the evaluation of the Investigation to be a distinct stage itself. An evaluation stage would not be expected in a Laboratory Report because the Experiment is assumed to have been set up by an 'expert'. However, this should not be confused with an evaluation of the results and we would expect students to suggest reasons or explain any unexpected results.

Patterns in the language

Perhaps the biggest and most obvious difference between the Laboratory Report and Investigation is at the language level: the former usually has orientations to the science rather than the scientist since it is a response to someone else's instructions, whereas the latter, because it is asking the student to take on the 'expert' role of scientist, typically has the student as the orientation.

This means that in Investigations, the student as scientist is in control, making decisions about how the method should be done and this pushes the meanings to be oriented to the 'one in charge' (e.g. 'I used two small seedlings' rather than 'Two small seedlings were used…'). The results stage, though, demands a shift to the results and so the writer changes orientation (e.g. 'The results across all three measurements were roughly the same…', '…the growth was quite erratic.')

Describing and organising

The purposes of these genres in science are concerned with representing the world in scientifically technical ways. They construct taxonomies of varying kinds, and they provide definitions and exemplifications of natural phenomena. They answer 'What is…?' kind of questions.

Descriptions

Text 4

Image: Jacob Spinks.
Accessed 16 Nov 2015 from commons.wikimedia.org

THE SEA EAGLE

Classification

The Sea Eagle (Haliaeetus albicilla) is a large bird of prey in the Accipitradae family. It is found all year round in an area covering large parts of northern Europe and northern Asia, as well as coastal areas of the continents in the Southern Hemisphere.

Appearance

The Sea Eagle has an appearance that makes it stand out. Overall, it is very large with a wingspan of around 2.5 metres and a length up to a metre. Its head is large and both its talons and beak are large and very powerful. The male, as in most birds of prey, is smaller than the female, with the female weighing up to 7 kg.

The adult Sea Eagle's body has a uniformly brown colour, while the head and neck are a slightly golden brown, the beak and eyes are yellow, and the tail is entirely white.

Diet

The Sea Eagle's diet is diverse and consists mainly of a range of seafood; for example, relatively small fish such as trout and large fish such as salmon. Almost any fish that is found near the water's surface is potential prey. The Sea Eagle also feeds on other sea birds; small mammals such as mice and rabbits; and carrion.

The Sea Eagle hunts for its food either by searching an area by gliding over it or by taking up a strategic position at a high point on land to scout the surroundings. Depending on the size of the prey, it is eaten by the Sea Eagle where it is caught or nearby, or it is carried in the bird's claws to the nest.

Breeding

Sea Eagles pair for life once a bond is formed after their territory has been established. A pair produces only one to three eggs per year, usually in early Spring. Both parents take care of the eggs over the 38 days before they hatch. The female is typically in charge of the brooding and feeding the chicks. It takes more than six months for the chicks to develop to the stage where they can be independent.

The Sea Eagle's nest is very large and remarkably heavy, about 500 kg. It is constructed with plant materials, such as large branches for the base and softer grasses and moss for the interior. The same nests are added to for many, many years, even by generations of Sea Eagles, and so can grow up to two metres in diameter. To allow for hunting and the safety of the chicks and to accommodate the size of these nests, they are typically located at the top of huge, well established trees or on the ledges of coastal cliffs.

Threats

Anything that threatens their nests and, hence, their chicks, or diminishes their food supply threatens the existence of the Sea Eagle. Therefore, logging, accumulated toxins in their prey because of pollution, hunting, egg stealing, intentional poisoning and even the blades of wind turbines can all pose major or minor threats to the Sea Eagle.

Patterns in the structure

The purpose of a Description is to describe multiple aspects or features of a natural or physical phenomenon. A Description typically begins with some kind of definition or classification as it locates the thing that is being described within some class or group.

The second stage in Descriptions is to present descriptive aspects. What differs from one text to another is what makes up that stage; that is, the sub-stages or phases. What we could say is that scientific texts typically have appearance as the first phase of this descriptive stage.

Why is the appearance phase immediately after the classification and is it obligatory to have it there? Keeping in mind that genres are examples of sociocultural activities that apprentice students into the discipline, we could say that the first two paragraphs are classification and appearance because that is how scientists organise their thinking and behaving. It is 'taken for granted' that the first thing a scientist does when meeting a new phenomenon or plant or animal is to try to locate it in the technical taxonomy that the scientist follows. They would ask, for example, 'What kind of organism is this?' To be able to classify it at the outset without doing, for example, any DNA tests, the scientist would look at its appearance.

The remaining phases in both texts are less pre-determined but it is still possible to argue why one phase might come before another. For example, diet could be argued to come before breeding because it is not only more easily observed but aspects such as how a bird hunts, what it hunts, how the food can be transferred and where the food can be stored determine, for example, where nests might be built and how big the nests have to be and who gets to look after the eggs and care for the young. Also, a typical pattern in Descriptions is that the more humans are involved, the further that phase is from the beginning of the text.

Patterns in the language

There are three main features of the language in Descriptions:

1. They are in the generalisable present tense, e.g. 'The sea eagle is a large bird of prey.'
2. The information is quite technical, e.g. 'The moon is a celestial body.'
3. The topic or aspects of the topic are the usual beginnings, e.g. 'Gold is shiny …'

These features are also true for the other describing and organising genres: Comparisons, Components and Classifications.

Why is there a lot of technical information provided?

Descriptions are typically used by experts to pass on their expert knowledge to others. We assume that these experts have done the experiments and research, and discussed with other scientists their findings and arrived at some point where they have knowledge that others would learn from. To transfer all their knowledge to a text, they need to use certain technical language.

Why are Descriptions in the present tense?

If the purpose of a Description is to describe multiple aspects or features of a natural or physical phenomenon, then we would expect that we are presenting generalisable information in the present tense. The information is not necessarily inarguable facts, but observations and assertions that were presented yesterday, that are similarly presented today and that will most probably be presented tomorrow. Descriptions in science that are in the past tense are those that are concerned with, for example, extinct species, e.g. 'Dinosaurs lived…'

Why are orientations of the meanings typically the topic of the Description?

The typical arrangement of information in writing in English is to have given information at the front (as the orientation) and the new information coming increasingly at the end. Since the purpose of a Description is to give new information about some scientific phenomenon, then we would expect the topic of the Description ('The sea eagle is ...') or some aspect of it ("The talons of the sea eagle are ...') to often come at the front as the orientation.

As students build their understanding of scientific concepts, they will shift the orientations from the concrete to the more abstract and technical. For example, young students will typically choose to write 'Sea Eagles eat a range of seafood', while older students will gradually be able to choose the diet of the bird as the orientation, 'The diet of the Sea Eagle consists of…'

At times, the orientations can be both abstract and technical: 'High electrical conductivity, malleability and ductility favour the use of gold in electronics…' instead of 'Because gold is malleable and ductile, and because it conducts electricity well, it is used for…'.

Comparisons

Text 5

COMPARING PLANT AND ANIMAL CELLS

On comparing animal and plant cells, we find that there are some major similarities and some critical differences. These differences are linked to the different functions that cells have in the different organisms.

Both animal and plant cells have three major structural elements: a defined nucleus, cytoplasm which surrounds the nucleus, and a cell membrane.

Plant cells also have chloroplasts and a large vacuole. A significant structural difference between the two kinds of cells is that the plant cell has a wall consisting of cellulose. This wall surrounds the cell membrane and allows the plant cell to withstand high pressure by taking in large amounts of liquid through osmosis without bursting. An animal cell, on the other hand, would burst if too much distilled water or other fluid filled it.

Patterns in the structure

If the purpose of a Comparison in science is to compare features of two or more physical phenomena, then Text 5 is just such an example, albeit a simple one. To achieve this function, it is organised so that the first stage identifies what is being compared, then it goes into the description stage with two phases: similarities, then differences.

An alternative approach would be, for example, to describe one of the cell types alone first so it acts as a 'control', and then compare the other cell type with the given. The discussion with the students would then be around which cell type they, as novice scientists, would choose to set up as the control.

One question to be discussed with students is whether the two phases have to be in that order: 'Would scientists find similarities first before looking at differences and why would that be the case?'

Patterns in the language

The main pattern is the language of comparison and, because of the approach by Text 5, words such as differences and similarities are chosen. Importantly, in terms of language development for students and what will be discussed later in the book as recycling of language, discussion of and around this text, as well as the text itself, will provide opportunities to use a range of words. For example, the text alone offers:

- similarities, similar, both have, animal and plant
- differences, different, differences...between, on the other hand

If the alternative approach to organising the text were to be used, then different language resources would be used. For example, once you have established the features of plant cells then, when it comes time to talk about animal cells, we would expect, for example:

- 'Animal cells do not have a cell wall. Instead of a cell wall, they have...'
- '...don't have a counterpart in animal cells...'
- '...not found in plant cells, while they are found in...'
- 'Although both have vacuoles, the vacuoles in animal cells are either absent or very tiny...'

Components

Since the purpose of a Component is to describe the component parts of an object or physical phenomenon, the layout typically has the verbal text describing the parts aligned closely with the visual text showing the parts, as we see in Text 6. It can happen that a Component is difficult to read if a complex verbal text were included alongside the visual and, in that case, we find that part of the verbal text is separated from the visual text. However, doing so demands a lot of the reader and, perhaps, the demand on the reader could be reduced by constructing more than one visual — a series of smaller Components.

Text 6

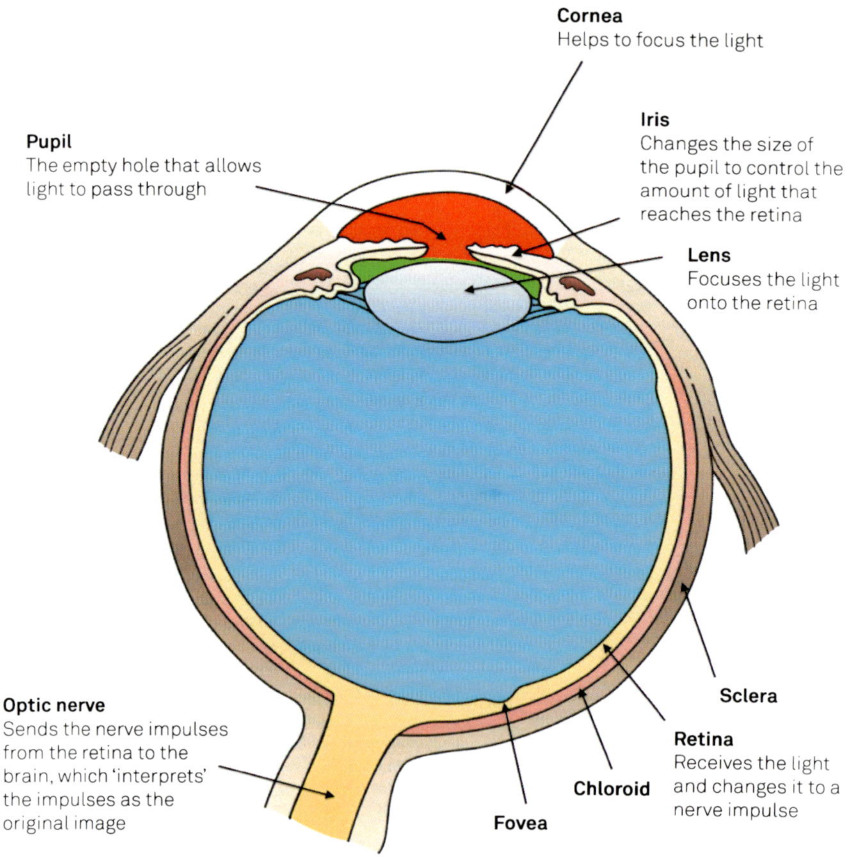

Original Image: Holly Fischer
Accessed 16 Nov 2015 from commons.wikimedia.org

Classifications

Whereas the relations in Components are whole : part (e.g. human eye : iris, cornea, retina…), the relations in Classifications are class : member of the class. This means that the organisation of a Classification sets up this classification, or taxonomy, as we see in Text 7.

Text 7

EARTHQUAKE WAVES

The energy that is released from earthquakes moves as waves. There are two main types of waves: body waves and surface waves and each of these types has two sub-types. Body waves travel through the Earth's inner layers, whereas surface waves move along the surface of the Earth.

Body Waves

One type of body wave is the primary wave, or P-wave, which is a compressional wave. Of all the seismic waves, the P-waves are the fastest moving and it is because they are the first waves recorded at seismograph stations, that they are called 'primary' waves. P-waves are able to move through all states of matter. These waves are longitudinal in nature, which means that, as the waves move out from the epicentre, the particles in the rock vibrate in the same direction as the wave is moving.

The second kind of body wave, called secondary waves, or S-wave, is a shear wave. Unlike P-waves, S-waves travel very slowly and cannot travel through liquids. S-wave particles move perpendicular to the direction of the wave.

Surface Waves

One kind of surface wave is the Love wave, which is named after the British mathematician, A.E.H. Love. It is the Love waves that typically cause the destruction of man-made structures such as buildings and bridges. They travel slowly from the epicentre moving from side to side but are slightly faster than the Rayleigh waves.

The second surface wave, the Rayleigh wave, also named after a British mathematician, produces the shaking experienced during an earthquake. These waves move like an ocean wave, both up and down and side to side in the same direction as the wave itself.

Patterns in the structure

As stated, a Classification's function is to set up a taxonomy according to class or type. Therefore, the structures that are discernible are taxonomies of classes, hierarchies, sets and sub-sets, groups and sub-groups. The actual text structure and the language together must set up the taxonomy. Figure 2 shows how Text 7 does that. Structurally, the taxonomy is realised through a layout and typography: at the top is the broadest heading with the largest lettering, the two kinds of waves discussed are then identified through subheadings with smaller lettering but still bolded; and then each sub-type of wave has its own paragraph.

Yet, there are patterns within the taxonomy itself for teachers and students to work with. Why are body waves placed before surface waves, and why do primary waves come before secondary waves and Love waves before Rayleigh waves? It appears that location is the first determining factor and then speed and magnitude of observable impact on man-made things are the next organising factors. Those closer to the epicentre are first-mentioned. In the body waves, the faster wave is the first mentioned. In the surface waves, the waves with the greater impact on the man-made world is first mentioned. If this is wrong, for example, whether the factor is really how the waves move, then an informed person (the teacher) needs to be able to explain what the more suitable order would be and why that is a more suitable arrangement, or why there is no special order. A deeper understanding of the field for the student and the teacher comes through this meta-awareness of the text's structure.

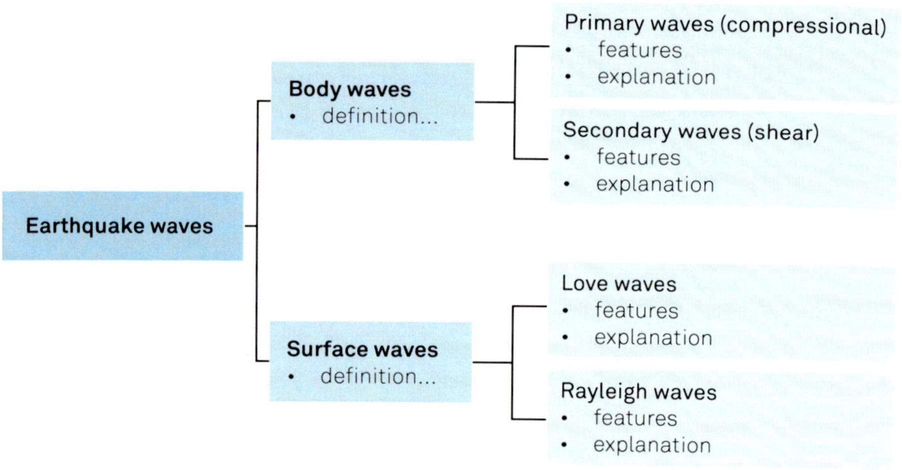

Figure 2: The taxonomic relationships constructed by Text 7

Explaining phenomena

The purposes of these genres in science are to explain, in technical ways, physical phenomena. They are a response to questions about how something happens or why something happens. The Explanations can be divided into two types, based on whether they are organised according to real time or not. If they are sequenced according to real time, they are called Sequential Explanations, whereas if they are not sequenced according to real time, then they are called non-temporal Explanations; specifically Factorial, Consequential and Theoretical Explanations.

Sequential Explanations are concerned with the cause and effect flow through a series of sequenced events constituting the phenomenon, such as: 'How do plants make their own food?' or 'Why does the solution change colour?' or 'Why does a coin in water look bigger than it actually is?' or 'How do tsunamis occur?' The Sequential Explanations are fundamental to science. It is not sufficient to know what something is but to know how and why something is the way it is. Although the structure may look relatively uncomplicated, it is the language that has to work hard to construct that apparent lack of complication. This has major implications for the teaching and learning of Sequential Explanations. It also has implications for the writers of textbooks and curriculum materials as well as teachers writing Sequential Explanations.

Non-temporal Explanations answer questions such as: 'What are the causes of diabetes?' or 'What are the causes of acid rain?' or 'What are the effects of acid rain?' or for a more complex example, both the causes and effects could be combined in one response, which would then be an example of a macrogenre. Texts that are oriented to the factors or causes of the phenomenon are called Factorial Explanations, while texts that are oriented to the effects or consequences of the phenomenon are called Consequential Explanations.

Sequential Explanations

Patterns in the structure

Sequential Explanations should always be able to be represented in some kind of flowchart. However, the images in the flowcharts are not sufficient in themselves. They represent the sequence of the text but do not tell us what the causal connection (varying in the explictness of the causal connections) is between the images nor express reasons why they are in that order. For that, one needs language.

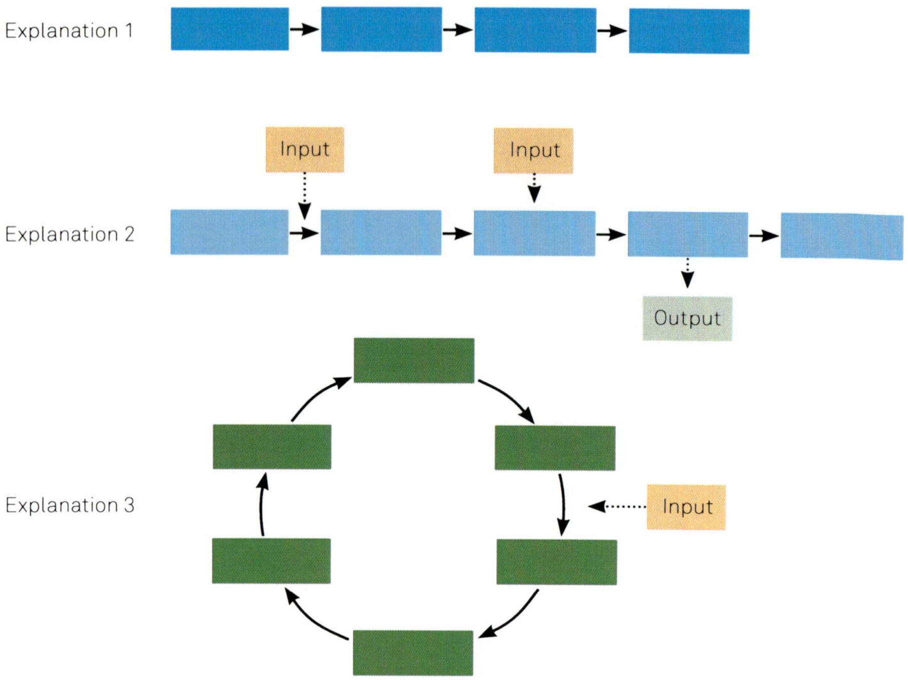

Figure 3: Examples of the flow of meanings in Sequential Explanations

The visual representations of Sequential Explanations typically unfold from left to right. This matches the movement of written texts in English and many other languages but clock movement as well, so that would mean that it would be preferable in terms of the demand on the reader for cycles to unfold in a clockwise direction.

Sequential Explanations have two stages: the phenomenon stage and the explanation sequence stage. Within the explanation sequence stage, there can be any number of phases as can be seen in 'The frog life cycle' (Text 8). There are minor variations in the literature: Unsworth (2001), for example, uses the term implication sequence for explanation sequence and states that there is an optional stage, too, named deduction or closure.

Text 8

THE FROG LIFE CYCLE

When frogs mate, the female lays eggs in water and the male sheds sperm over the eggs to fertilize them.

About one to three weeks later, the eggs hatch into tadpoles, which breathe using their gills and move like a fish with their long tails.

By the time they are about 6 weeks old, the external gills have disappeared and the tadpoles begin to develop lungs.

Around two weeks later, the tadpoles form hind legs, their bodies become longer and their heads become more distinct and more frog-like.

After about 12 weeks, the almost mature froglets start to grow front legs and lose their tails. Their lungs are fully developed for breathing.

Eventually, the mature frog has lost its tail completely and, as an adult, is able to live on land.

The phenomenon stage identifies the phenomenon that is going to be explained and very often it simply functions as the title of the text, such as: 'How the bionic eye works', 'Water cycle', or 'The frog life cycle'.

The explanation sequence is where the real work of this genre happens. In Text 8, the phases within the explanation sequence could be identified, starting with the adult phase and followed by the egg-laying phase and so on. What is highlighted in bold face are the time elements that help sequence the phases — this will be discussed more fully in the next section. In terms of the complexity of the phases, the more technical the field, the more likely it is that there will be many phases and even phases within phases.

Text 9

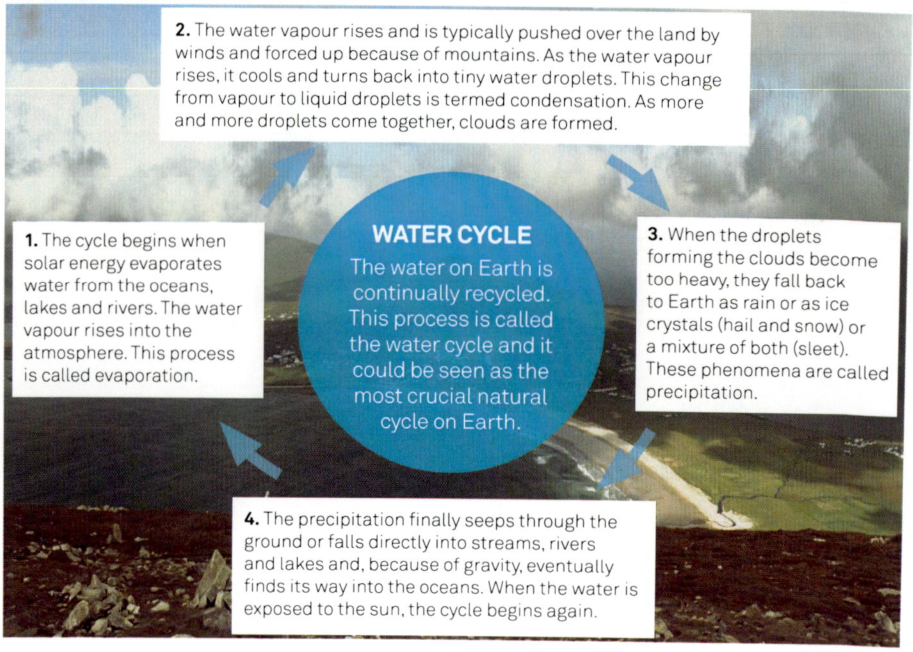

Patterns in the language

There are several main features of the language in Sequential Explanations:

1. They are in the generalisable (simple) present tense, e.g. 'The eggs *hatch* into tadpoles', 'The water vapour *rises* …'

2. The actions and the objects involved in the physical phenomenon in Explanations can be technical but, generally, their purpose is not to define technical meanings but rather to focus on the processes of the phases involved. The process being explained is typically an abstraction of varying degrees of technicality (e.g. life cycle, oxidation).

3. The text unfolds as a flow of information, where the product of one action often provides the beginning materials for the next action, which continues the process. For example: 'Female frogs lay **eggs**. **The eggs** hatch to form **tadpoles**. **The tadpoles** grow…'. This is even more obvious if we use 'which'. For example: 'Female frogs lay **eggs**, **which** hatch to form **tadpoles**, **which** grow…' More specifically, in order to construct the flow,

the orientations of the meanings (i.e. the front of the clauses or clause complexes) are typically taken from the new information presented in the previous action.

4. They may also have elements of time such as temporal conjunctions (when, as, after), dependent clauses of time ('when frogs mate'), and circumstances of time (around two weeks later) — the 'Frog Life Cycle' text has identified in bold italics those elements of time that come at the front of a phase.

5. Causality in Sequential Explanations can be expressed along a cline of explicitness — each text varies in terms of how explicit cause is expressed (compare the greater explicitness of Text 9 with Text 8). If causal meanings are explicitly identified, then these will be expressed using, for example: causal conjunctions (because), causal processes (results in, produces), causal circumstances (due to, because of), and causal nominals ('The effect of this is...', 'The outcome is...').

Note that of the five features mentioned in this list, it is the third feature that is specific to Sequential Explanations.

Why are the orientations in Sequential Explanations patterned the way they are?

The pattern is necessary for the language to create the flow of actions in the text. The common pattern is for new information presented in the previous phase to provide the beginning (the orientation) for the next phase. This feature will be taken up in greater detail in the sections on language.

Factorial and Consequential Explanations

Non-temporal Explanations of the factorial and consequential kind answer questions such as: 'What are the causes of acid rain?' or 'What are the effects of acid rain?', respectively. Or they could simply have the phenomenon to be explained worded as 'The factors that influence the moment of inertia', or 'The consequences of air pollution for Hong Kong' or simply, but ambiguously, as 'Deforestation'.

Explanations that are oriented to the causes or factors responsible in the phenomenon are called Factorial Explanations, while texts oriented to the effects or consequences of the phenomenon are called Consequential Explanations. As we saw for Sequential Explanations, there can be any number of phases within each stage. The structure of these genres is quite straightforward: they begin with the phenomenon and then simply list the causes or effects. Typically, the most significant causes or effects are the first mentioned.

Theoretical Explanations are similar in structure to the Factorial and Consequential Explanations but their purpose is to illustrate a theoretical law or principle. So, we would expect the law or theory or principle to be defined or described in some way and then, in the explanation sequence stage, we would see examples of applications of the law, theory or principle.

Factorial Explanations

Text 10

WHAT ARE THE FACTORS THAT INFLUENCE THE MOMENT OF INERTIA?

The moment of inertia of a body is a measure of the resistance to changing the rate of rotation. The equation for moment of inertia is given by $I = \sum mr^2$. In simple terms, this equation shows us that the moment of inertia depends on two factors: the mass of an object and the distance of this mass from the axis of rotation. We can see this illustrated in any activity in which humans are spinning or tumbling, such as ballet dancing, figure skating and diving. For example, as figure skaters spin or pirouette and they draw in their arms, we can see them increasing their rate of rotation. By drawing in their arms, they are decreasing their moment of inertia and, since angular momentum is conserved, their rate of rotation increases accordingly.

With her arms extended from her body, the skater increases the mass distribution around the central axis of rotation.

Bringing in her arms reduces the mass distribution around the central axis of rotation, as if the skater's arms have now formed a column around her body.

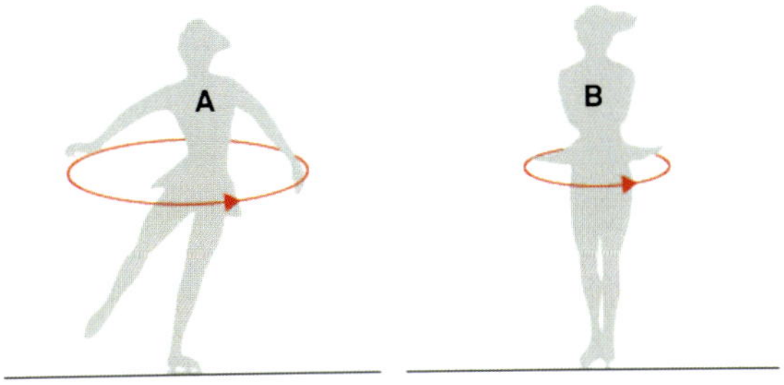

Assume that:

- only the skater's arms are moving in and out as she is spinning
- the mass of her arms does not change
- the span of her arms when extended is greater than when wrapped tightly around her body.

Which moment of inertia is greater?

We know	I	$=$	$\sum mr^2$
Given	m_A	$=$	m_B
and	r_A	$>$	r_B
then	$\sum_A mr^2$	$>$	$\sum_B mr^2$
ie	I_A	$>$	I_B

Consequential Explanations

Text 11

Image: Tokyoahead at English Wikipedia
Accessed 27 Nov 2015 from commons.wikimedia.org

WHAT ARE THE CONSEQUENCES OF AIR POLLUTION IN HONG KONG?

Air pollution is increasingly a major problem for cities around the globe, and Hong Kong is no exception. Air pollution can be defined as the presence of airborne particles that are harmful to the well-being of animal and plant life. The quality of life in Hong Kong is negatively affected by air pollution in several ways and they include: rising temperatures, degradation of visibility, acid rain and depletion of the ozone layer.

Rising temperatures are the major result of the greenhouse effect, which, in turn, lead to droughts and increasing sea levels. The greenhouse effect is the name given to the atmosphere behaving in the same way as a greenhouse, which allows certain radiation to enter the glasshouse but stops other radiation escaping. More precisely, objects on the earth absorb UV light and emit low-energy infrared radiation, which is trapped by the earth's atmosphere, resulting in increased temperatures. The effect is worsened when the atmosphere is concentrated with air particles and/or pollutants such as water vapour, carbon monoxide, carbon dioxide and methane. Hong Kong will be greatly affected by at least one of the suggested consequences of increased global temperatures and that is the rise in sea level caused by the melting polar regions. With much of Hong Kong hugging the coastline, any rise in the sea level would be disastrous for urban areas and food supplies as fish populations and farming areas are adversely affected. Also, the impact of hotter and extended summers on the health of Hong Kong's elderly citizens will be an increasing concern.

Visibility degradation is caused by airborne particles which scatter light and serve as condensation nuclei for clouds and fog. The particulates can come from natural phenomena such as volcanic eruptions, dust storms and sea spray, or from human activities such as combustion. In Hong Kong, the combustion of fossil fuels in cars is the main contributor and the situation is worsened by the occurrence of photochemical smog, which is formed when smoke and exhaust fumes are trapped in a fog and undergo photochemical reactions.

Acid rain is a chemical phenomenon caused by the dissolution of nitrogen oxides and sulphur dioxide in rainwater to form nitric acid and sulphuric acid, respectively. The oxides are released during the combustion of fossil fuels by cars, factories and power plants. Acid rain has multiple adverse effects on ecosystems, where plants and soils are degraded, and on humans and property. Irritation of respiratory systems and corrosion of buildings and car bodies are some of the ways acid rain afflicts the people of Hong Kong.

The depletion of the ozone layer reduces the protection from harmful UV light that the ozone layer provides humans. The ozone layer is between 12 km and 50 km above the earth's surface and is being depleted by chlorofluorocarbons (CFCs), which react to break down the ozone. Although attempts have been made to replace CFCs, they are still widely used as solvents, refrigerants and aerosol propellants. Reducing the concentration of ozone will lead to greater amounts of UVB reaching the earth. This may cause problems such as skin cancers, eye disease and gene mutation.

In Hong Kong, air pollution is monitored by the Environmental Protection Department and its many initiatives have resulted in positive outcomes, although further improvements can be made.

Theoretical Explanations

Text 12

ARE WATER AND OXYGEN ESSENTIAL FOR IRON RUSTING?

Rusting is the formation of iron oxide and both water and oxygen are essential for the rusting process. If either water or oxygen is absent, no rusting occurs. If both water and oxygen are present, iron rusts and forms hydrated iron (III) oxide, which is reddish brown.

This test uses iron nails in three test tubes with varying combinations of water and air.

Test tube 1	iron nail is immersed in anhydrous calcium chloride without water	with air
Test tube 2	iron nail is immersed in boiled distilled water with a layer of oil on top	without air
Test tube 3	iron nail is immersed in distilled water	with air

The observations show that only the iron nail in Test tube 3 turns reddish brown, while those in Test tubes 1 and 2 do not. This shows that rusting requires both water and air.

■ (Polias 2008b)

Patterns in the structure

While the structure of the Sequential Explanations follow a time sequence and can be presented as flowcharts, non-temporal Explanations are organised as the phenomenon being made up of several parts. They could be seen as having structures that look like a nucleus (phenomenon) with several satellites (phases in the explanation sequence but not organised according to time). These structures (Fig. 4) are referred to as orbital structures (Iedema et al. 1994).

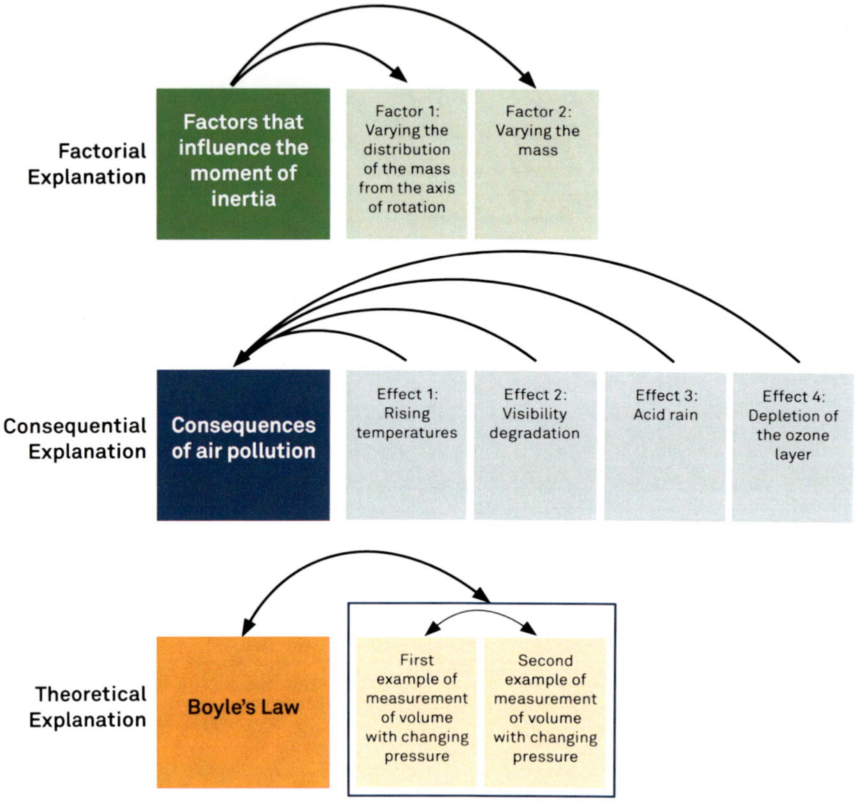

Figure 4: Orbital structures of non-temporal Explanations

Arguing

Arguments are becoming increasingly common in science curricula as the ethical and moral issues of the application of scientific research and knowledge become more openly discussed. In school science, the fields that tend to be argued about are those that deal with societal, medical or environmental issues.

There are two main types of arguing genres. One kind presents one point of view and they are the 'Agree-with-me' and 'Agree-with-me-and-take-some-action' Arguments. The second kind presents multiple points of view on an issue and they are called Discussions. Text 13, which is an example of a Discussion, could be changed into an example of an Argument by altering the topic to, say, Nuclear power cannot solve our energy problems or Nuclear power is still a viable solution to our power needs.

As the 'agree-with-me' suggests, that sub-genre of the Argument genre attempts to persuade the reader to accept a particular position on an issue as the most valid. The 'agree-with-me-and-take-some-action' sub-genre is not only concerned with getting the reader to agree with the writer but to take some action as well.

Arguments do not attempt to balance the pros and cons of an issue, no matter how controversial the issue may be. On the other hand, Discussions do not argue for one position, but instead balance two or more positions on an issue as if they are 'weighing up' evidence in an objective, rational way before passing some kind of judgement or, possibly, a recommendation at the end.

Discussions require more extensive knowledge of the field. They are viewed by science teachers as more important than Arguments because they illustrate the scientific principle of continually testing an idea, refining it and researching it and, therefore, taking care not to have a strong opinion on something.

Discussions

Text 13

CAN NUCLEAR POWER HELP ANSWER OUR ENERGY NEEDS?

Nuclear power attracts diametrically opposed viewpoints: its advocates see it as relatively inexpensive and sustainable and a way to combat global warming, while its opponents see its waste as so toxic and long-lasting that it is a threat to the planet.

With respect to the emissions of greenhouse gases, nuclear power is a clean way of producing electricity when compared with coal-fired power stations, which currently meet most of the world's electricity demands. If the projections of the effect of global warming due to increased carbon dioxide emissions are correct, then nuclear energy is an antidote to consider carefully. Also, the fuel it uses, uranium, is more abundant than fossil fuels and much, much less is needed to produce the equivalent amount of energy.

Nevertheless, even though nuclear power stations produce fewer greenhouse gases than fossil-fuel power stations, they do present contamination risks to the planet with emissions of radioactivity and, more significantly, with the disposal of waste and accidents at the power plants. Nuclear waste requires very special treatment and storage methods so that the risks of the radioactive waste are minimised. However, despite all the planned precautions, human carelessness and natural disasters have caused very serious accidents at nuclear plants. For example, the explosion in the Chernobyl nuclear power plant in 1986 in the former USSR was due to human factors, while, more recently, in 2011, a human disaster was initiated by a natural disaster, a tsunami, at Fukushima in eastern Japan. The impact of both events have been catastrophic for their regions and will continue to be for a very long time.

Many major accidents have also happened in the mining of fossil fuels and in the production of power from those fuels. It is the case that many more people have died from the negative consequences of fossil fuels than from nuclear power (New Scientist 2011). So why are people so fearful of nuclear energy? Perhaps it is the fact that deaths from fossil fuels occur in smaller numbers over a long time whereas nuclear accidents tend to be catastrophic. Also, the high level of toxicity of the by-products of nuclear energy length and the time they remain toxic makes many think it is too great a risk to take. In order to make nuclear power and the storage of the waste material safer, expensive research and development is needed. This cost would be too great for many developing countries where capital and technology are limited. But even in affluent, developed countries, safety is still a major concern, as the Fukushima catastrophe shows.

Nuclear power seems to have various advantages. It is relatively sustainable, efficient, clean and inexpensive. However, at the same time, the waste issues still hinder its development as a major and common source of power. Fossil fuels that currently fire the majority of the power plants are not a viable long-term option either due to global warming. In the long run, therefore, it seems that renewable alternatives to the use of both radioactive fuels and fossil fuels offer solutions to future power needs.

Patterns in the structure

Arguments and Discussions consist of three stages: the thesis or issue, the arguments, and reinforcement of the thesis in light of the information presented. Each of these usually also consist of phases.

The thesis stage (Arguments) or the issue stage (Discussions)

The thesis stage in an Argument functions to introduce the issue in question, to state the writer's position on the issue, and to preview the aspects of the topic to be taken up. The compulsory stages would be:

- stating the issue and, in an Argument, indicating in some manner the position taken
- previewing the arguments to be made or issues to be taken up.

In a Discussion, the first is the issue stage where the issue is stated and various aspects of the issue are previewed. The writer should not have an opinion on the issue at the outset.

With this stage in both genres, there may be a number of phases, such as identifying the significance of the issue in science or society, or placing the issue in its historical context.

The arguments stage

These are the arguments that were previewed in the thesis or issue stages. In an Argument, it is through these arguments that the writer aims to convince the reader to accept a particular position on an issue or to act in a particular way. In a Discussion, these are the aspects of the issue to be taken up and the writer has to be seen to be balanced.

Arguments and the discussion of the issues need to be substantiated in some way. This could be by providing some research evidence or it could be by building up a case through 'scientific knowledge'. For example, if one wanted to talk about why sunscreens should be compulsory for children playing outdoors at school, then an Explanation about how UV rays actually do their harm to human skin might be used. This would push the text into an example of a macrogenre and it would typically be used in the years of schooling when students can understand the science of skin cancers but can also research complex tests.

Many strong examples of Arguments often include the opposing views, not to applaud them but to denigrate them. By putting their arguments down, they are in effect promoting their own. Rather than seeing this as a stage, the inclusion of opponents' arguments would be considered as phases in the arguments put forward by the writer. The opposing viewpoints or evidence are essential in a Discussion and the writer has to be careful to present them in an unbiased fashion.

The reinforcement of the thesis

In an Argument, the purpose of this last stage is to re-affirm the thesis stated in the first stage but in light of the evidence presented in the arguments stage. It is the last call to agreement and so is often interpersonally loaded but, importantly, there is a major difference between the beginning stage and the final stage of an argument. With the thesis stage, the reader has not yet read the text and so it must prepare the reader for what they will read, hence the previewing of the arguments and, often, the historical contextualisation. However, by the time the reader has reached the reinforcement-of-the-thesis stage, they have read the text and so the function of this last stage is twofold: to restate the thesis once more but in a more 'interpersonally loud' manner, and to support this restatement with the new information presented in the arguments. If there is a call-to-action phase in an Argument, it usually comes in this stage.

In a Discussion, the function of this stage is more of presenting a deduction or an evaluation of the issues and evidence presented in the Discussion.

Patterns in the language

There are many varied language resources used to persuade. The following list provides some features of more persuasive texts.

- 'Factual' knowledge would usually need to be referenced to specific research or experts to make this knowledge persuasive. We will see later how scientists also avoid making bald assertions by expressing degrees of certainty. In other words, they construct themselves as open-minded scientists who problematise, test, and hypothesise and are still "not sure", rather than as people who simply accept something as fact and do not undertake further testing.
- The language needed in a Discussion for presenting a more balanced consideration of the issue include conjunctions of comparison: 'Compared with'; 'However'; 'Nevertheless'; 'even though…' But there also needs to be a wide range of resources for hedging or tempering meanings: 'seems to have', 'will', 'cannot', 'potential risks',

'likelihood'.

- Appealling emotionally in Arguments: 'a waste of resources', 'a shocking waste of resources', 'with tragic results'. Often, it is not just through a single word such as 'shocking' but through fragments of attitude and emotion in words that accumulate their intensity through the text. Of course, it does not have to be highly amplified in emotion. Many examples of Arguments choose a much more neutral way of appealing to the reader because they believe their persuasive ability does not come from being emotional but from being seen as objective and rational with significant evidence to support them.
- In 'agree-with-me-and-take-some-action' type of Arguments, there needs to be some expression of obligation, eg: 'Always wear sunglasses to protect your eyes', 'Doctors advise us to wear sunglasses to protect our eyes', 'It is advisable to wear sunglasses to protect your eyes'.

Acknowledging scientists

Most science curricula include the requirement that students learn about the history of science and they generally do this by focusing on the scientists who were the prime architects of theories or those who were the major researchers in a scientific breakthrough. The genre that allows for the appreciation and documentation of research into a person's personal and professional history is the Biography.

Biographies

Text 14

ALBERT EINSTEIN

Albert Einstein, born in Ulm, Germany, in 1879, is recognised as the founder of theoretical physics because of his very significant contributions to science, including the theory of relativity, explanations for the motion of particles in fluids and the photoelectric effect. His fame is such that, if people were asked for the name of a scientist, the first and possibly only one they could mention would be Einstein.

Einstein wasn't very much interested in school and showed no special scholastic ability at all but, even as a small boy, he was fascinated by the natural sciences and independently immersed himself in studying scientific literature. He attended secondary school in Switzerland and graduated from the Swiss Polytechnic Institute in 1900. He had some tutoring and part-time teaching positions for a couple of years and then succeeded in gaining a position as examiner at the Swiss Patent Office.

1905 was a significant year for Einstein. He was awarded his doctorate at the University of Zurich but, importantly, 'Annals of Physics', a German scientific periodical, published three of his papers, each of which would contribute enormously to science. The first paper explained the motion of particles in fluids. The second explained the photoelectric effect, and the third paper was on his 'Special Theory of Relativity'.

Between 1909 and 1914, Einstein held a number of positions as professor in prestigious European universities: professor of theoretical physics at the University of Zurich; professor at the German University in Prague; and professor of physics at the Berlin Academy of Sciences, as well as director of the Kaiser Wilhelm Physical Institute. He was also elected to the Prussian Academy of Science in Berlin in 1913.

In 1916, Einstein's 'General Theory of Relativity' was published. Then, five years later, at the age of 42, he was awarded the Nobel Prize for physics for his explanation of the photoelectric effect and not for the theory of relativity since, at the time, relativity was still rather controversial.

The increasingly anti-Jewish actions in Nazi Germany in 1933 led Einstein to decide to stay in the USA, which he was visiting at the time. He joined the staff of the Institute for Advanced Study at Princeton, New Jersey. In 1939, on the eve of World War II, he alerted the US president that Nazi Germany might be experimenting with nuclear fission and recommended that funding be made available for similar research. As a result of the research, the first atomic bomb was dropped to end World War 2 in 1945.

The use of nuclear energy for military ends greatly disappointed Einstein and in the years after the war, he worked very hard to seek some world agreement on control of its use. In addition, as a man with a deep compassion for politically and economically oppressed people, he supported the idea of a world government.

Albert Einstein's contributions to science led to the development of the quantum theory and, consequently, to a better understanding of matter and energy, in particular, nuclear energy. This great man died in Princeton in 1955.

Patterns in the structure and the language

The stages in Biographies are:

- orientation (who, location and significance)
- record of events (all of these are in chronological order)
- reorientation (a reiteration of the significance and possibly contextualisation in some future).

The tense is in the past and, importantly, the sequence of events is achieved through a timeline and this timeline typically has elements of time at the front of the paragraphs. Once the signal for the new event has been made, say, at the start of the paragraph, the orientation is back to either the person being written about or aspects of that person's life. We can see both these points in the following extract:

> "1905 was a significant year for Einstein. He was awarded his doctorate at the University of Zurich but, importantly, 'Annals of Physics', a German scientific periodical, published three of his papers, each of which would contribute enormously to science."

Macrogenres

So far, we have explored the range of genres in science that have the capacity to function as elemental or prototypical genres. As the meanings in science become more and more complex, the activities become more and more complex, and so the prototypical genres are exploited in complex macrogenres. A macrogenre can be defined as a genre complex; a genre that is made up of combinations of any number of the prototypical genres.

We will now look at several macrogenres to see how these genre complexes are formed. Also, we will see that the more detailed and technical (and abstract) the scientific knowledge becomes, the more likely it will need a macrogenre to make the meanings adequately.

Description with Sequential Explanation

Text 15

MINING METHODS AND PROCESSING

The mining of gold occurs either deep in the earth's crust or in open-cut mines. Underground mining is used where the depth of ore below the surface makes open-cut mining uneconomic. Vertical shafts and declines (spiral tunnels) are used to move people and equipment into and out of the mine, to provide ventilation and for hauling the ore and waste rock to the surface. In open-cut mines, large earth-moving equipment is used to remove waste rock from above the ore body and then to mine the ore. The waste and ore are blasted to break them into sizes suitable for handling. The waste is transported to dumps and the ore is taken to the crusher. The crushed powder is mixed with water, the gold sinks and the other wastes are washed away. The gold is treated with chemicals, and melted and purified in a process called smelting. In this process, base metal impurities are oxidised and absorbed, leaving the precious metals to be poured into ingot moulds. The smelted gold is then refined.

The extract (Text 15) from a Description on gold has a short Sequential Explanation (identified in red) included within it so as to explain the processes involved in open-cut mining. This is a kind of zooming in or out of describing so as to concentrate on explaining. Once the explaining is over, the text goes back to describing.

Consequential Explanation with Sequential Explanations

Figure 5 presents three consequences of deforestation (making up a Consequential Explanation) within which there are Sequential Explanations explaining each outcome of deforestation. The flow in the Sequential Explanations is illustrated using arrows so that the outcome of one event acts as the beginning of the next event. It is common in science to have quite short Sequential Explanations, which means that they often feature inside other genres, thus making macrogenres.

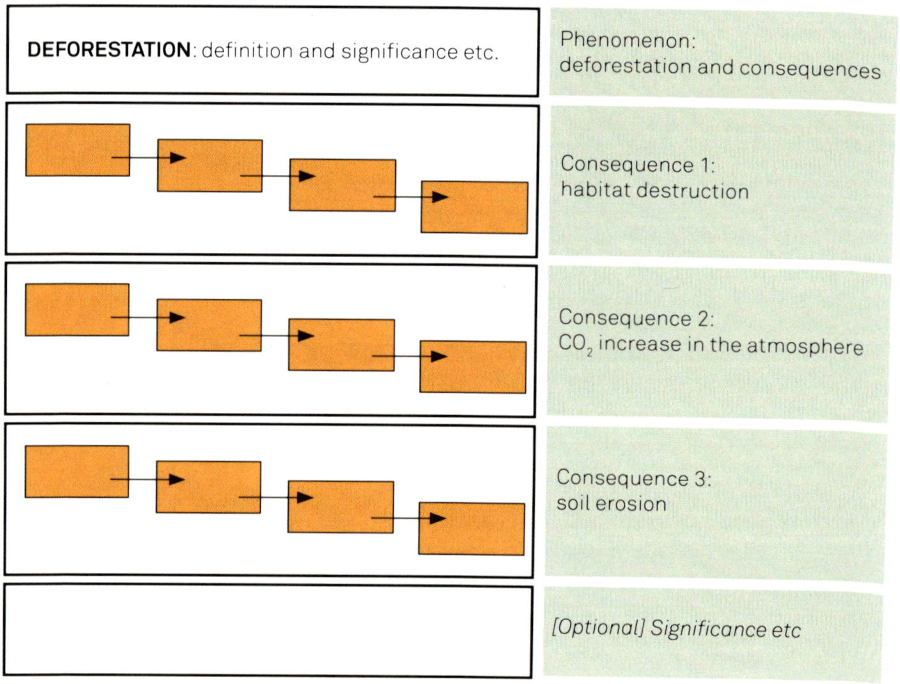

Figure 5: A schematic representation of Sequential Explanations within a Consequential Explanation (Polias 2007a)

Figure 6 represents one of the Sequential Explanations (How deforestation causes erosion and what effect that soil erosion could have) inside the Consequential Explanation (Fig. 5). The visual representation of the Sequential Explanation shows that it is complex to a certain degree. But there is further complexity in understanding whether flooding is an effect of erosion or a cause or whether it is both an effect and a cause of further erosion and, if so, how it is visually represented? The complexity that is possible in Sequential Explanations underlines the linguistic and non-linguistic challenges faced by teachers and students and why it is necessary to consider carefully the teaching of them so that learning is maximised.

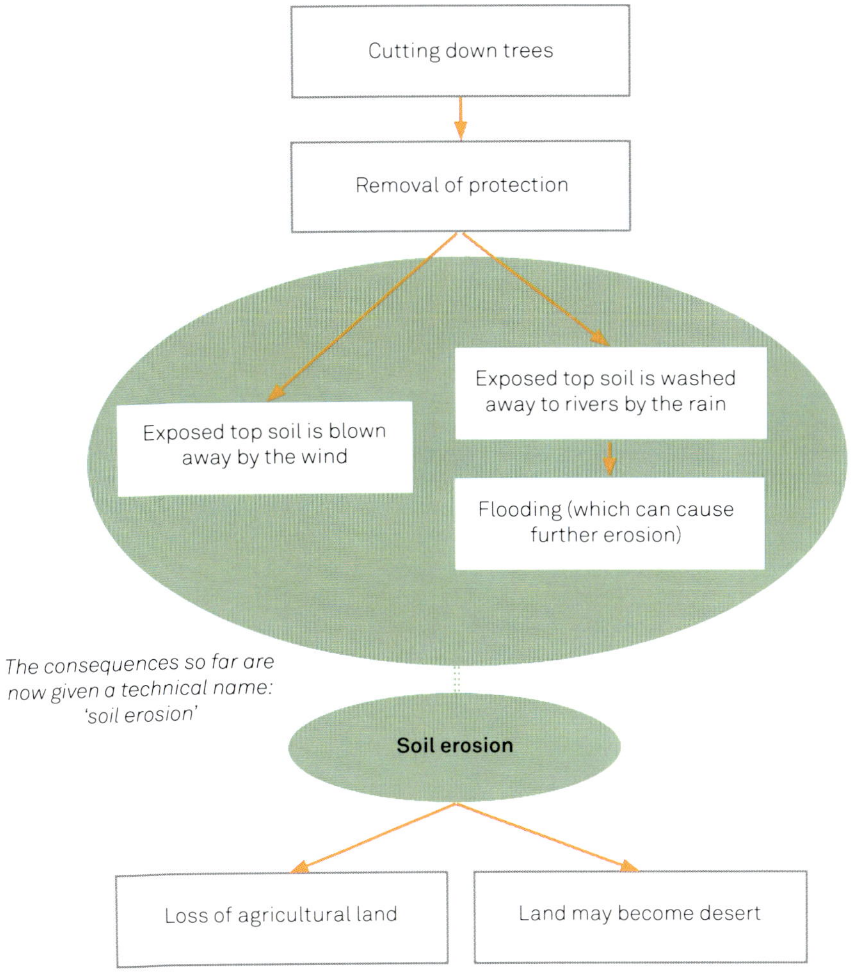

Figure 6: A visual representation of a Sequential Explanation (Polias 2007a)

Figure 7 is one example of a student text from the class that had worked on deforestation. The worksheet provides a sentence starter as support for the student although this kind of support was removed in the latter stages of the lesson. The real success of the student's text lies its being the outcome of the scaffolding that the teacher provided in the lesson through visuals and interactions.

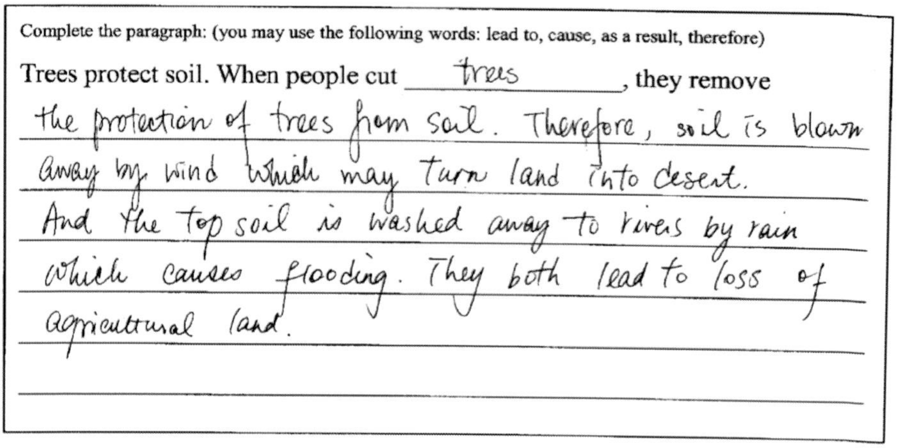
Complete the paragraph: (you may use the following words: lead to, cause, as a result, therefore)

Trees protect soil. When people cut trees, they remove the protection of trees from soil. Therefore, soil is blown away by wind which may turn land into desert. And the top soil is washed away to rivers by rain which causes flooding. They both lead to loss of agricultural land.

Figure 7: An extract from a student text on the effects of deforestation (Polias 2007a)

Multiple ways of making meaning

Scientists do not construct science through verbal texts alone but rather through complex combinations of the various meaning-making resources available; in other words, multi-semiotically.

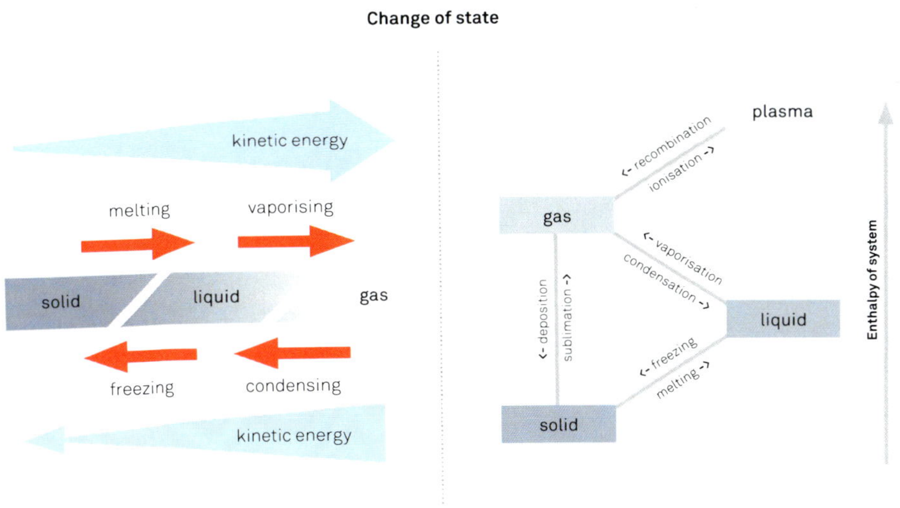

Figure 8: Diagrams that can be animated to provide multiple access points

Figure 8 presents two options for presenting states of matter, each one with its own advantages and disadvantages depending on the age of the students and what they have been taught beforehand. In both, the arrows can be animated when working in the classroom. In the simpler model, the three states of matter are on a cline (illustrated by the shading) in an attempt to show that the changing states are aligned with the changing kinetic energy, although there are still three separate states and hence the divisions between the three states. In the more complex model, the arrangement of the states of matter in a triangle allows for the direct changes between gas and solid to be explained clearly whereas that would be confusing in the simpler model. While the teacher is using spoken language and written language (the labels on the visual), gestures are probably used as well in an attempt to complement the work of the animated arrows. For the students, having the visuals animated at the same time as the teacher's language and the hand movements mirroring the meanings is a small example of pedagogical resonance, which occurs when the ways in which the teaching itself happens resonate with the patterns in what is being taught.

Text 16

HOW DOES THE HUMAN EAR WORK?

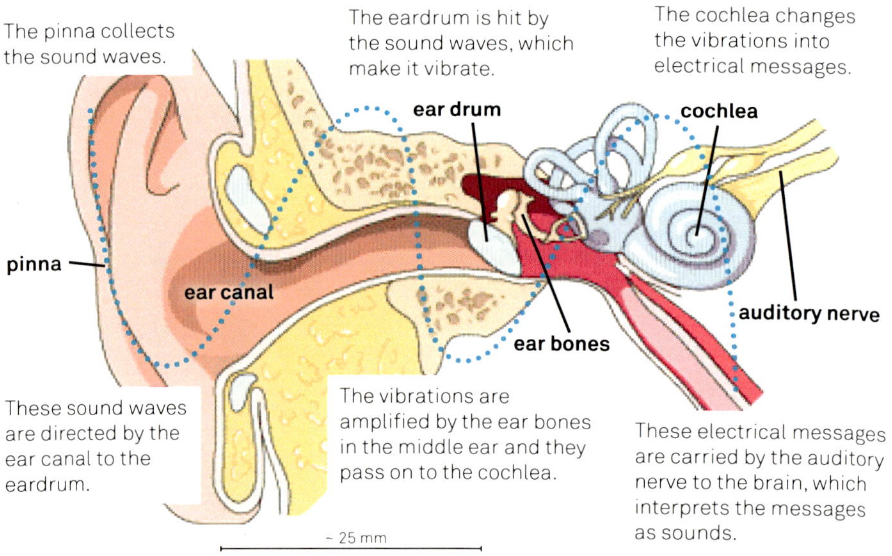

Text 16 is a macrogenre (Component with Sequential Explanation) that has a number of visual meanings that could be brought to students' attention:

- The phenomenon stage is placed above the visual text and

the scale of the visual is placed clearly underneath the explanation sequence

- The cross-section and, therefore, the verbal text is read from left to right, which mirrors how English is read
- Lines pinpoint the location of the components of the ear
- The verbal text is split into 6 parts, with each part corresponding to a phase in the explanation sequence
- Each phase of the verbal text is situated adjacent to the relevant location in the ear so that it is easy for the reader to read both the visual text and the verbal text at the same time, as if the invisible process of hearing is made visible.
- The dotted blue line, which is drawn in by the teacher, shows the flow of the text. This could also have been done by numbering each of the six phases to make it clear to the reader in which order they need to be read.

Summarising the main meaning-making systems in science

With visuals, we can consider whether they are the real thing, a photo of the real thing, or a diagram of the real thing. For example, is the student observing a real plant cell under the microscope, talking about a photo of a real plant cell or is it a diagrammatic representation of a plant cell as seen under a microscope?

We can ask if the visuals or verbal text are animated and what kind of animation. Are there simulations or time-lapse photos or videos and are they unfolding in real time? It is the limitations of traditional technology that often make it difficult to make sense of dynamic processes in phenomena. For example, words on a page do not easily represent the phases in the process of germination in the same way a simulation by video would be able to do, or in presenting the pedagogical movements of a teacher and students as they attempt to explain, through the use of their bodies, how the human ear works. It also does not allow for 3D modelling and rotation through the model so it is possible to see the object from any number of points of reference.

Further, we can ask:

- Is the visual a diagram, a graph, a table or an equation? Is the visual a cross-section and from which perspective is the cross-section taken?
- Is colour used and what meanings do they realise, e.g. is colour used to differentiate oxygenated and deoxygenated blood?

It is especially in Sequential Explanations, where dynamic processes are attempted to be recontextualised in classrooms that we need a good understanding of the range of visual resources that are available and an understanding of how they work.

In later sections, we will be examining written language in detail but we can still be alert to the fact that language is not just what is seen on the page but, in spoken language, is also about sound, or the phonological elements such as intonation, rhythm, stress, and pace. This is especially important when considering a teacher's delivery but also when we look at the pronunciation of the technical words in science, many of which have links to Greek or Latin, and also when identifying which syllable to stress in a word; for example, óxidise and oxidátion, (photo)sýnthesis and synthétic.

Signposting the content of a unit of work

With an increasing tendency to not rely on a single textbook or even any textbook and instead to access multiple information sites, there is an increased risk of students losing sight of where they are headed in their learning. It is not unusual for adults, when setting out on some new path of learning, to research what is likely to be learned, both broadly and then more specifically in lessons or over a series of lessons. Students in schools should be treated no differently. They need to know where they are going and not go forward in their learning 'blind'. Previously, one could have pointed to the indexes in their textbooks or chapter contents lists, and students and teachers could have continually referred to the main sections as they were about to start on them or in revising their work. As mentioned, this may not be possible with changing technologies for accessing information.
So, one way of providing this overall picture of how the knowledge is going to be sequenced and organised is what I am calling signposting. Figure 9 is an example of one kind of overarching graphic that teachers and students could work through, examining it at the outset and then referring to it and marking it off as each section is completed. It starts with a definition of corrosion, including different kinds (wet and dry) and examples of what corrosion is and, as the diagram shows, it moves through to explanations of the processes involved in corrosion, then moves into writing down the chemical reactions and then preventing corrosion. Within this unit of work, any number of genres could be enacted.

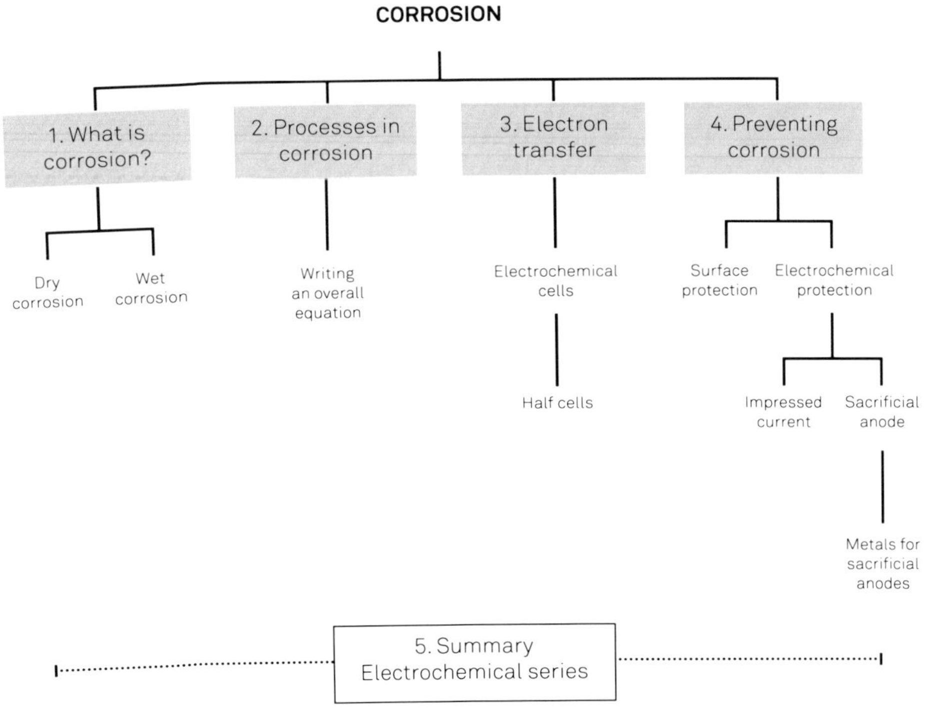

Figure 9: Signposting for students the sequence and organisation of a unit of work on corrosion

Consolidating scientific behaviour

In this section, we revisit some of the genres and see that the development of these by students and, hence, their development as apprentice scientists can be scaffolded by teachers' pedagogical choices in further examples of pedagogical resonance.

Older students, who are asked to follow the safety protocols of laboratories, are usually asked to put on their lab coats. It is clear to them that they are taking on the role of apprentice scientist. However, with young students, whose laboratory is often the same classroom in which they study their other subjects and so do not wear lab coats, it is not as clear. Moreover, their teacher is usually not a science teacher but their class teacher, who not only teaches them science but their other subjects as well. So, there is no demarcation in location or personnel to signal to the student that they will now be behaving like 'scientists'. For young children, a simple way is to ask them to put on caps that have the label 'Scientist' attached to them and explain that, when wearing those hats, they will be behaving as scientists.

In addition, confusing messages are sometimes given to students when they are asked to evaluate or comment on their 'research' in some way. The task can push them to respond with expressions such as 'I enjoyed learning about sharks but I'd be scared if I saw one'. If we are apprenticing students into the world of science, then this evaluation shifts them into taking a non-scientific role. To reduce that risk, the wording of the evaluating questions needs to focus on the science, e.g. 'What aspects of sharks do you need to research further?'

Describing and organising

Having discussed the reasons for the stages and phases in the Description on the Sea Eagle being organised the way it is, we can use this so that there is resonance between its organisation and how we teach our students to construct a similar text.

In Figure 10, the note-taking framework for the Description matches the unfolding of the technical knowledge about the bird. The vertical layout (rather than horizontal) matches what the final text will look like on the page. Even if it were placed on a website, the information ought to be organised so that the reader is led through this unfolding. A reader can choose to go to a specific place in the information and start reading but they would usually not do that the first time they start to learn about the Sea Eagle. It is more likely that they choose to do that when they are researching specific details of the bird. Of course, this is so not only for this text but for any text of the Description genre.

What kind of bird is it?
Classification

What does it look like?
Appearance

- an appearance that makes it stand out
- very large with a wingspan of around 2.5 metres and a length up to a metre.
- large head and both its talons (claws) and beak are large and very powerful.
- adult male smaller than female: female weighs up to 7 kg
- uniformly brown colour
- head and neck are a slightly golden brown
- beak and eyes are yellow
- tail is entirely white.

What does it eat?
Diet

How do they breed and care for their young?
Breeding

What are the things that threaten them?
Threats

Image: Jacob Spinks

Figure 10: A note-taking framework for a Description on the Sea Eagle

Even though this is called a note-taking framework, it ought to be used at the outset, when the students and teacher are embarking on their exploration of the Sea Eagle. That is, the work on the class board and class discussions are guided by the questions that construct the Description rather than allowing for an unguided free-for-all of contributions. This is important because, by engaging in the guiding questions in the order they come in the text, the students are apprenticed into the scientific ways of behaving. If we began by viewing a film of the Sea Eagle or, if fortunate enough, to see an actual one, we would focus on what we observe in terms of its appearance, habitat and, possibly, behaviour. From there, we would need to move to some reference material that tells us what ornithologists have already classified, and compare our observations with the documented reference material so that we can classify it. We would then move, hopefully through videoed illustration, to its diet and eating habits because, again, they are easily observable. The next phases in the generic activity, such as breeding, are less easily observed by students and this is where language (perhaps the narrator of the video clip) plays its important role; it provides information that has been researched by others and is not readily observable or researched by the student or novice scientist.

Explaining phenomena

The interplay between the verbal text and the visual text is crucial to understanding the processes in Sequential Explanations. The patterns in the verbal text will be discussed in detail later in the sections on language. At this point, it is necessary to point out that it is not simply static visuals that we need because the processes being explained unfold according to real time. What is needed is typically a simulation of the actions in the process. Construing meanings of dynamic phenomena is very difficult to do through language alone so the use of time-lapse photography of actual events or videos of actual events and/or simulations whose movement can be slowed or paused is vital. Of course, looking at moving images does not explain the process; one needs language for the processes to be explicit and that is why we need to look at language as well.

Recounting events in a scientist's life

When working with Biographies, most timelines are given as a series of events strung out horizontally. The problem with this is that it doesn't look like the way that it is to be documented by a student writing on a page or on a screen, where paragraphs move vertically on the page rather than horizontally. Figure 11 shows what it can look like vertically (Polias 2010). The advantage of the vertical orientation is that it is much easier for a teacher and students to convert the individual dates to verbal expressions of those times and time periods (the second column) and connect them to the notes they have in the third column to formulate the sentences that make up those paragraphs.

ALBERT EINSTEIN'S LIFE

1884-1903	**... in school**	• interest lay in natural sciences • secondary and tertiary education (1900) in Switzerland • tutor, then examiner at Patents Office
1905	**1905 was ...**	• doctorate • 3 main papers published: motion in fluids, photoelectric effect, General Theory of Relativity
1909-1914	**Between 1909 and 1914, ...**	• number of professorships • director of KWPI • elected to PACS in Berlin in 1913 ...
1916	**... in 1916**	• General Theory of Relativity published
1921	**Then, five years later, ...**	• awarded Nobel Prize for Physics for photoelectric effect

Figure 11: A timeline for a Biography orientated vertically

A model of language for educators

So far, we have been examining patterns of meanings in the activities and texts that construct the knowledge comprising school science and these should not have been unusual to science teachers who have 'grown up' with these activities and texts. The perspectives might have been new but what we actually looked at would not have been new. However, if we are to really understand these patterns and implement this understanding in the classroom, we need to have tools for the analysis of the meaning-making resources that constitute these patterned scientific meanings. Since the primary meaning-making resource for us as humans is language, we will use a model of language that has proven itself to be useful in this regard for educators. This model is Michael Halliday's systemic-functional model, a model of text in context.

The systemic-functional model (Halliday & Hasan 1985, Halliday & Matthiessen 2014) sees language as a social meaning system, where text is situated in context. However, genre-based pedagogies have led many practitioners to accept the merging of genre theory and systemic functional linguistics theory and the resultant model (Halliday & Martin 1993, Martin 2012, Matthiessen 1993) is illustrated in Figure 12. From the model, we could conclude that every text reveals some information about the situational context itself and the cultural context in which that language is used; in other words, the context shapes the text. However, every text has the potential to shape, even in minute ways, the context, so the vector between context and text is two-headed: context shaping text and text shaping context.

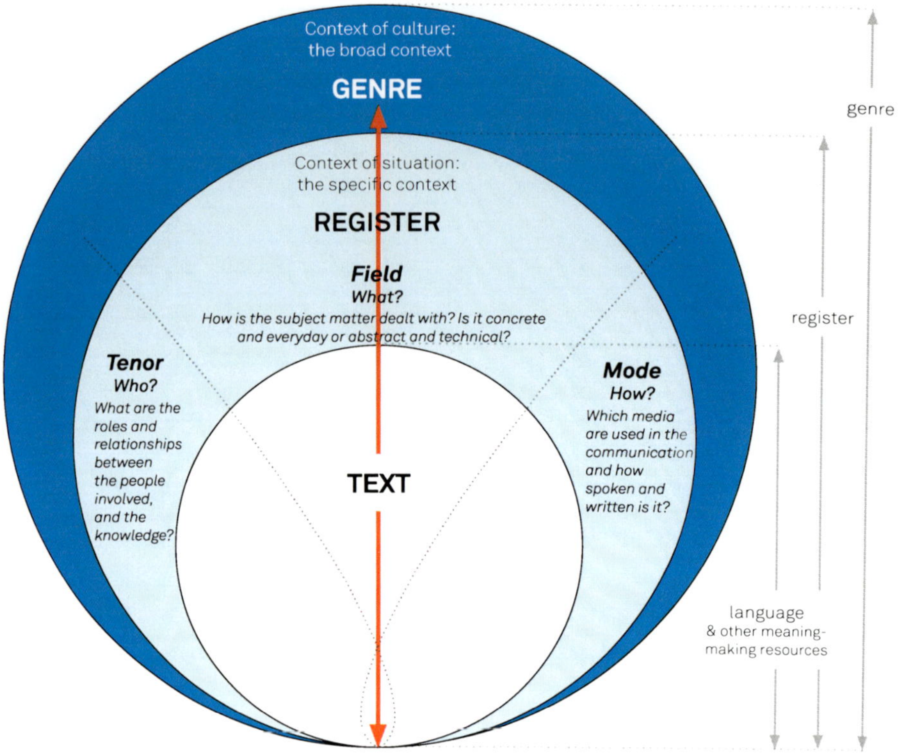

Figure 12: The systemic-functional model of language incorporating genre

Context is the non-verbal environment of the text. It is made up of two parts: the broad context of culture and the more specific context of situation. For the purposes of this book, it is helpful to link context of culture with genre, the patterned and predictable ways of getting things done. The context of situation, the specific context within the broader cultural context, is identified through the three variables that constitute the situation: field, tenor and mode. Any configuration of these three variables is called the register. Previously, the patterns of structure and the patterns of language in the various genres of school science were presented. Focusing now on register will allow us to understand more about the patterns of language that realise meanings in science. We will consider each of the three variables in more detail, since register has a significant pedagogical contribution to make. For a discussion of the language development in school-aged students in science, refer to Christie and Derewianka (2008). For a language-based developmental continuum across the curriculum for school-aged students, refer to Polias (2003).

Register

Field

Field can be seen as the representation of the topic from a particular perspective. For example, if the topic were cheese, then a scientist would be using content words that are of a certain degree of technicality, such as: 'lactic acid', 'bacteria', 'somatic cell counts', 'microbiological quality' rather than the content words chosen by a consumer of cheese, such as: 'hard', 'soft', 'ripe', and 'smelly'.

Fields vary in degree of technicality and abstraction. Figure 13 plots this variation along a continuum. At one end, fields are concerned with the concrete, commonsense or everyday; in the middle they are specialised with minor degrees of abstraction and technicality; and at the other, fields are highly technical and abstract.

Field and the other two register variables are realised by certain linguistic (and other semiotic) resources, as we will see.

Tenor

Tenor is concerned with the interpersonal elements of the context and varies along a continuum from a high degree of subjectivity and informality to a high degree of objectivity, formality and expertise. The aspect of tenor teachers of science would be most interested in would be the degree of expertise and willingness to be seen as a member of a professional community. This determines, for example, what degree of certainty the writer chooses to use. This is important when students are interpreting their results in experiments; for example, how do they express how certain they ought to be about the conclusions they draw from their observations, especially when they compare them with the observations and results of countless other researchers? Tenor is also concerned with whether there is a need to include other, expert voices.

Mode

Mode refers to the role of language itself: does it play an accompanying role in the text or does it constitute the text itself? Additionally, it is concerned with the medium of communication in any situation, which affects how a text is organised and how it flows. As for the other two register variables, mode can also be seen as occurring along a continuum, from spoken to written. At one end of the continuum, there is the most spoken language, which usually happens face-to-face (e.g. doing the steps in Experiments) and accompanies some kind of action. In the middle of the continuum, spoken and written language overlap — some texts are written but are easily read aloud, such as texts in which there is instructing or recounting what was done in the experiment; other texts are spoken but could easily be written such as short Sequential Explanations. At the other end of the continuum, language is most reflective and most written, where the text is constructed by the writer for an unknown reader (typically in school this 'unknown' reader is the 'known' teacher), and deals with generalisations and abstractions, such as in Classifications, non-temporal Explanations, and the discussion and conclusion stages of a Laboratory Report.

In addition, the use of any communication technology will have a bearing on the role that language plays together with the technology. This is clear if we consider what would happen if a life cycle was explained first in words only and no visual, and then explained with visuals added, and then with the use of animation.

Register continuum

Register distinguishes one example of a genre from another of the same genre: one configuration of meanings from another. Success in learning can be seen as developing control of a variety of genres and registers; the more genres and registers a student has developed some control of, the more likely it is that he or she will be or is perceived to be successful.

Within a unit of work, we are often moving students along the register continuum (Fig. 13) from the commonsense, concrete end of field to the technical, abstract end. At the same time, we are doing the same for the tenor and mode continua: moving from subjective to objective meanings, and moving from spoken language accompanying action to written language as reflection, respectively. We will use this continuum in the next section to help us consider macro-scaffolding and meso-scaffolding.

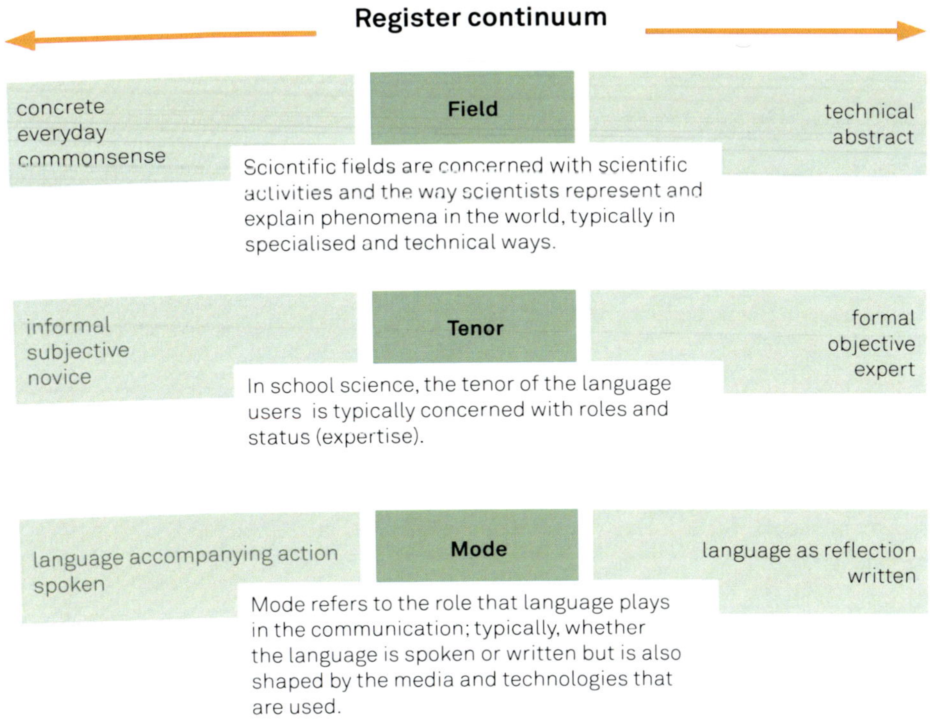

Figure 13: The register continuum

The internal organisation of language

Moving out of the context now and into language, Figure 14 represents how each of the three contextual variables is linked to the language. This is the significant feature of the systemic-functional model; it links language systematically and directly with context. Here, Halliday is using the term 'functional' not in the sense of external functions — where language is useful for various generic purposes — but in the sense of language's own internal functions. These internal functions are the way the language systems are organised to make meanings; in other words, to get the job done. So, according to the Hallidayan model, language has functional groupings that realise field, functional groupings that realise tenor and functional groupings that realise mode — all operating simultaneously. The functional groupings that are of most value for science teachers and their students will be taken up in detail in the remaining part of the book. These include the functional groupings that enable students to:

- express the increasingly technical and abstract meanings of science
- make sure texts are organised and flow well
- construct themselves as critical-thinking scientists.

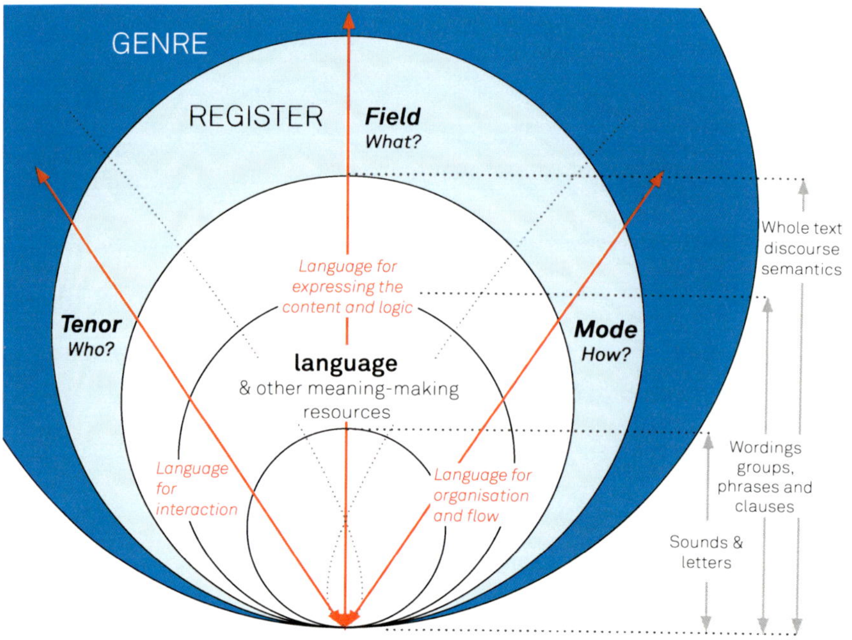

Figure 14: The internal functions of language related to context in the systemic-functional model

Scaffolding in the science classroom

Macro-scaffolding

Having examined the range of educational science genres and begun to consider register, a method of implementing this new understanding in a way that scaffolds students is needed. One way is to organise activities in the classroom so that they provide a natural progression along a genre and register continuum; in other words, a macro-scaffold (van Lier 2004, Hammond 2001, Sharpe 2001). A macro-scaffold also sets up opportunities for scaffolding at lower levels: meso-scaffolding and micro-scaffolding (Wood et al. 1967, van Lier 2004).

Figure 15 shows one possible macro-scaffold, moving from action to explanation without human agency; in other words, from the congruent to the more technical and abstract. By definition, a scaffold is only that if it is successful, so what are the features of the sequence of genres and registers as designed in Figure 15 that make it successful and, hence, a macro-scaffold? To start with, the first genre for the students to work with is one in which the grammar and lexis (words that carry content) are as simple as possible. The method stage of an Experiment (Text 17) fits these demands because the instructions ('Take a small green leaf from a healthy plant') can be seen as being expressed through simple grammar (imperative mood), and the lexis is typically of concrete things and actions ('Take', 'small green leaf', 'healthy plant'). Not only that, but the method stage of an Experiment can also be observed and understood with relatively little language if a teacher exploits available visual resources. This means that the answers to the questions a teacher can ask about the activity are readily available to the students. For example, if watching a video of someone doing something, the questions could be:

- (about the action) What's she doing?
- (about who or what is involved) What's she boiling?
- (about where, when and how the action is happening) Where's she boiling the water?, How long is she dipping it in the water for?'.

Text 17

EXPERIMENT

To test for starch in a green leaf

Method

1. Take a small green leaf from a healthy plant.
2. Boil some water in a beaker and then turn down the Bunsen flame.
3. Use forceps to dip the leaf into the boiling water for about one minute.
4. ... and observe any colour changes that occur.

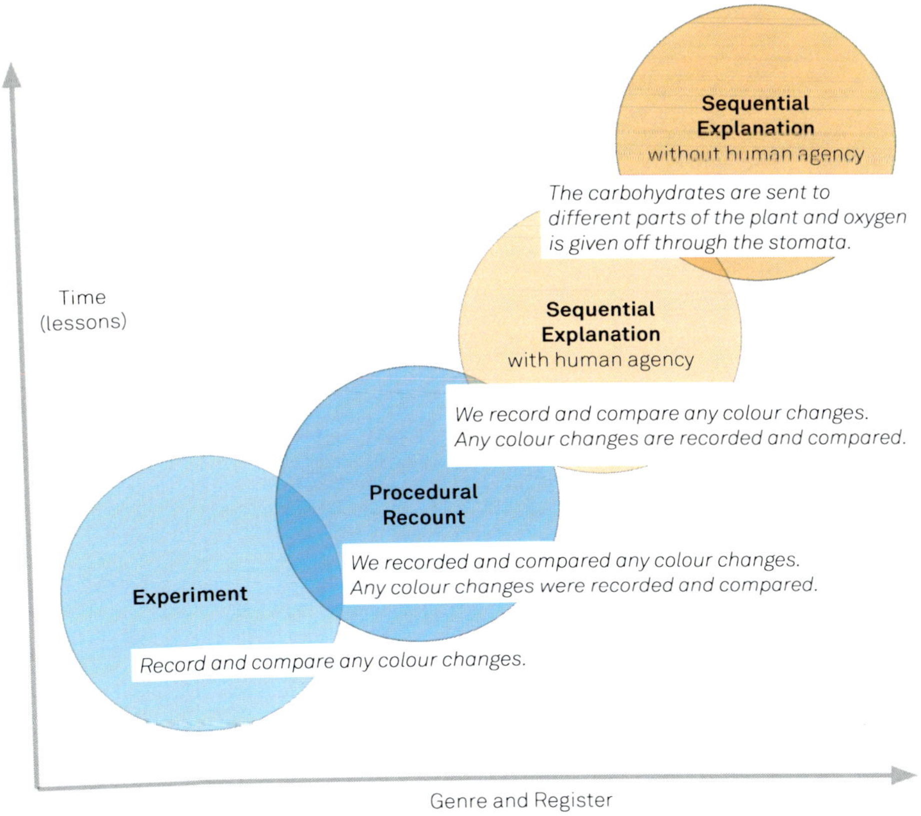

Figure 15: A sample macro-scaffold moving from Experiment to Sequential Explanation

The next genre, Procedural Recount, is helpful in providing a macro-scaffold because the lexis remains the same and only the grammar changes. In other words, the clauses are now statements ('We took a small green leaf from a healthy plant') rather than commands and the tense is in the past. Having the lexis unchanged helps the students because they can concentrate on the actions they carried out, which are not distant memories and hence easily retrievable, and any technical words are also easier to recall since they would have them written down as part of the method stage they had just completed. The main choice for the teacher (and then the students) is whether the text from the students is a response to "What did you do?' (Text 18) or 'What was done?' (Text 19) in the Experiment. Text 19 also requires the student to have control of the passive voice ('were observed'). A simple yet highly successful way of teaching the passive voice to students is taken up later in the book.

Text 18

LABORATORY REPORT

Method *(as Procedural Recount with the orientation to the scientist)*

We took a small green leaf from a healthy plant and dipped it in a beaker of boiled water for about a minute. Then we took out the leaf and pushed it to the bottom of a large test-tube water.

...

Lastly, we dropped iodine solution over the entire leaf and observed any colour changes.

Text 19

LABORATORY REPORT

Method *(as Procedural Recount with the orientation to the 'science')*

A small green leaf from a healthy plant was dipped in a beaker of boiled water for about a minute. Then the leaf was taken out and pushed to the bottom of a large test-tube water.

...

Lastly, iodine solution was dropped over the entire leaf and any colour changes were observed.

The next phase in the macro-scaffold is to move into Sequential Explanations. However, to go from a Procedural Recount to a Sequential Explanation without human agency would be risking too big a shift in register so a Sequential Explanation with human agency (Text 20) is designed into the sequence of genres. Text 20 expresses how scientists, in general, test for starch in green leaves and to do that it uses the simple present tense to make those generalised meanings. The difference in the language resources between Text 20 and Texts 18 or 19 is simply that the tense is different: past tense for the Procedural Recounts ('we dropped iodine solution' or 'iodine solution was dropped') and present tense for the Sequential Explanation ('we drop iodine solution' or 'iodine solution is dropped'). It is this small, manageable increase in demand on the language user that functions as a macro-scaffold.

Text 20

EXPLANATION

How is starch in green leaves tested?

A small green leaf from a healthy plant is dipped in a beaker of boiled water for about a minute. Then the leaf is taken out and pushed to the bottom of a large test-tube water.

...

Lastly, iodine solution is dropped over the entire leaf and any colour changes are observed.

The last Sequential Explanation is without human agency and is the kind of Sequential Explanation that explains how physical phenomena occur; for example, how photosynthesis occurs in a plant. These are the kinds of phenomena that typically cannot be observed while they are happening and this is even more so in schooling. Generally, scientists work from post-event observations or from testing of the products of events, and then they generalise from those after having studied many examples and having compared other scientists' work. This is very difficult for students to do in school contexts and yet they are required to do so at the end of the Laboratory Reports in the discussion and conclusion stages. The language resources needed to write these generalisations (e.g. "The carbohydrates are sent to different parts of the plant and oxygen is given off through the stomata") are, as the register continuum outlines, not developed in everyday communication and, hence, there is the need for a macro-scaffold.

Meso-scaffolding: shifts in register in classroom interactions

We have discussed shifts in the form of macro-scaffolds using genre and register, and we will also look into micro-interactions or contingent scaffolding (Wood et al. 1976); that is, the scaffolding that happens at the point when the student's brain is primed to take on the challenge of learning or, using Vygotsky's (1963) term, working in their zone of proximal development. However, if we accept that scaffolding is on a cline between macro-scaffolding and micro-scaffolding (Figure 16), then there ought to be a semantic space that sits between these two endpoints. The cline or continuum is one based on how planned or contingent the scaffolding is and so shifts between highly contingent and highly planned. Using van Lier's (2004) term, we can call this meso-scaffolding. Note, however, that the definition here differs from that given by van Lier, who sees it more as a lower level macro-scaffolding. Meso-scaffolding, as defined here, is more concerned with register than genre and lies somewhere between macro-scaffolding and micro-scaffolding and varies according to how contingent and how planned it is. The more planned it is, the more it is like macro-scaffolding. The more contingent it is, the more it is like micro-scaffolding.

Meso-scaffolding is, perhaps, best understood through how it is achieved and what it does. It can be achieved through incremental shifts in the register by taking small steps backwards and forwards across the register continuum in the myriad interactions that happen in the unfolding of a lesson. In each step is an associated shift in language, a shift that we want to be not so great that it is not accessible to the students but challenging enough for there to be new learning. Typically, the general shift is from the left to the right of the register continuum so the meso-scaffolding's ultimate purpose is to move students to the right on the continuum, to be able to make the abstract and technical meanings necessary to behaving as a scientist. Of course, teachers choose activities that move students left and right along the continuum as they plan for or react contingently to the needs of their students but the primary function of meso-scaffolding is to develop in students the language resources that shift them to being able to express the meanings further right along the register continuum.

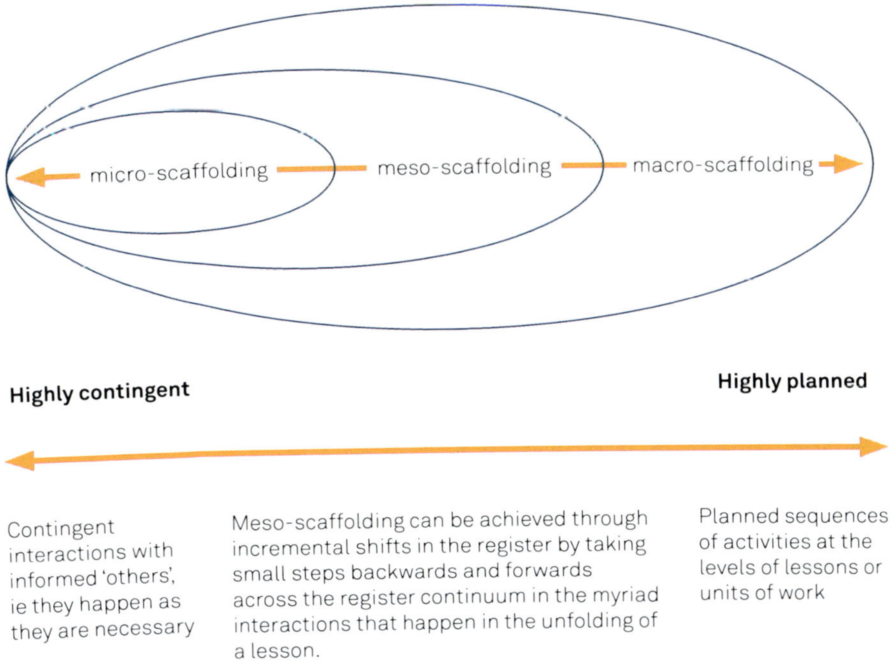

Figure 16: Scaffolding on a cline from highly contingent to highly planned

How can we plan for meso-scaffolding or, even if we have not planned for it, how can we implement it contingently or spontaneously in a lesson as a reaction to what is happening in the classroom? A simple way for teachers being alert to this shuffling across the register continuum is to consider three variables: people, space and time (Polias 2008a). Increasing each of these three variables changes the register so that it either shifts to the left, towards the highly spoken end of the continuum, or it shifts to the right, towards the highly written end of the continuum. So we can move the language to the right on the register continuum by:

- increasing the number of people involved in the communication
- increasing the space between the people involved in the communication
- increasing the period of time between when something is happening and when it is talked about.

Clearly, changing more than one of these variables at a time shifts the register to a greater extent than changing only one variable at a time. Being alert to this means that teachers can prepare for this but also be ready to make modifications if too big a shift has inadvertently occurred and the students are finding difficulty with the task at hand or, conversely, are finding the task not challenging enough.

Changing any of the meaning-making media in the classroom (PowerPoint, pointer, written text, video, objects) would also impact on the register of the activity but how the language changes depends on what media are used and how and when they are used. This is in contrast to the other three variables, which typically change the language in a predictable way across the continuum.

We will use a description of activities in a physics lesson (Polias 2006) and then use transcripts from a biology classroom to show what typically happens when there are changes in people, place and time, and media.

Register shifts in a physics class

Prior to the lesson being discussed here, the class had studied three aspects of physics — the effect of impurities on changes of state, the behaviour of light, and inducing an electromagnetic force (emf) — and the students were asked to design an experiment on each of the three aspects.

Figures 17, 18 and 19 are visual representations of the relationships that are afforded by each situation in the lesson as it unfolds. The magnitude of the arrows (vectors) indicates how much is contributed to the various parts of the lesson by the teacher and students.

Step 1

At the start of the lesson, the teacher goes over the content that the students need for their activities.

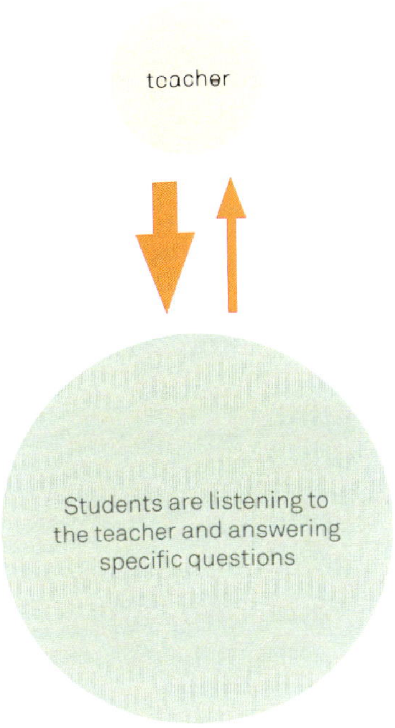

The teacher is in control of the transmission of information and does most of the talking. However, the questions asked by the teacher are expected to be answered in an extended way by the students. The teacher continues to elaborate and extend but also asks for clarification, explanation and reasoning. In this way, the students are provided with a lot of information by the teacher but are also involved by the teacher. This means that when it comes for the students to do the task the teacher sets, they are clear about the content of the task and the process of the task.

Another important aspect of the way the teacher supports the students' learning is the way he 'unpacks' technical terms, e.g. by talking about inducing or creating or producing an emf after he introduces the abstract term, induction. His questions to the students then allow them to use 'induce' before they use 'induction'. This interplay between abstract noun and more concrete verb and back to abstract noun is effective in scaffolding students' development of the concept, their ability to use it to discuss solutions to problems and also their ability to read and write more complex and technical texts.

Figure 17: The beginning of a lesson with the teacher taking on greater control

With the teacher being in control and with the students responding to specific questions, we could predict that the context probably lies somewhere closer to the midpoint of the register continuum: an expert teacher with informed students, with the teacher talking about the field in specialised and, to some degree, technical ways, and producing quite extended passages of talk without interruption from the students. The language in this specific context, even though it is spoken, has a lot of similarities with the language of writing. Now, if this 'lecturing' continued for a lengthy period of time, one could say that the demand on the students as listeners would typically be too great and they would probably stop listening at some point. The teacher has understood that and constructs a different context in the lesson, which is Step 2.

Step 2

The students have now been organised into three groups and been instructed to design an experiment. One group is to work with impurities and the melting point of ice, another is to design an experiment on the behaviour of light and the third is to work with inducing an electromagnetic force.

The role of the teacher has shifted from the controller of the input to the knowledgeable contributor to the group discussions. The task demands that the students negotiate their group's design, using the language needed for information-giving, reasoning, explanation and clarification.

Group work, such as this, allows students to be involved in negotiating meaning, using whatever language levels they have. Since working face-to-face with their peers is less demanding than standing up in front of the class as an individual, it allows them to explore their understandings of the topic in a more interactive way.

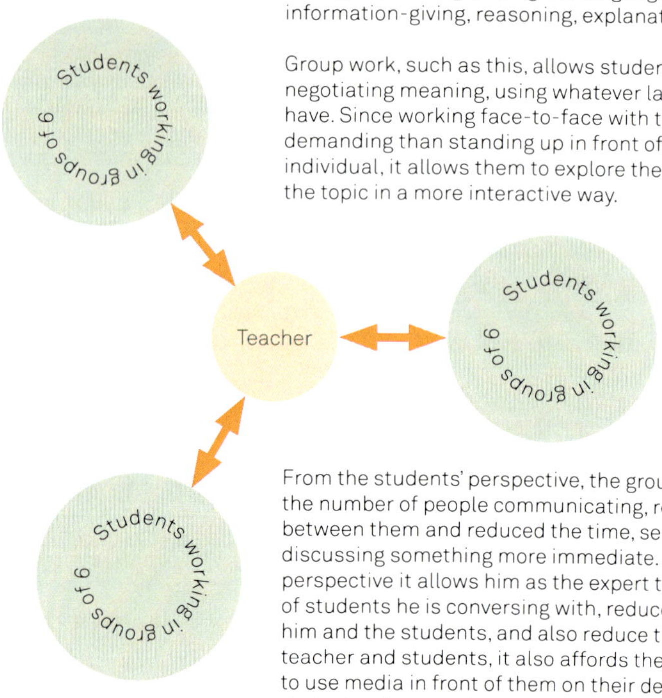

From the students' perspective, the group work has reduced the number of people communicating, reduced the space between them and reduced the time, seeing as they are discussing something more immediate. From the teacher's perspective it allows him as the expert to reduce the number of students he is conversing with, reduce the space between him and the students, and also reduce the time. For both teacher and students, it also affords them the opportunity to use media in front of them on their desks as they go about designing the experiments.

Figure 18: Group work as the students now take on much more control

In this configuration, the register has shifted to the left on the register continuum although each group will be different in terms of the register; the knowledge, the power relationships and the possible use of various media vary. The teacher is available to all three groups and is afforded opportunities to shift the register in any way that is necessary to scaffold the students. Significantly, he can still take on the role of teacher — perhaps instructing, perhaps challenging the students by posing questions, perhaps evaluating the students' contributions, or perhaps by simply staying silent and listening — but he is also afforded a different role and that is as a co-contributor.

Step 3

After the three groups have collaborated to design their experiments, the students come to the front of the class in their groups and report to the class on their design for the experiment.

All of the students in the group are at the front of the class, even though they have chosen one student to initially be the reporter. This allows any of the students to respond to further questioning from the teacher and other students.

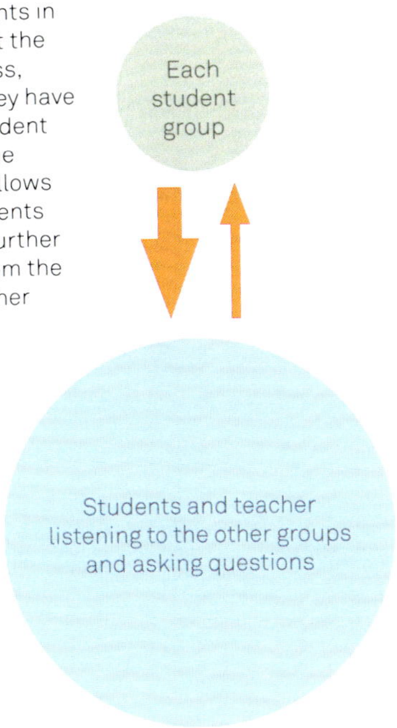

The task shifts the register to the right and demands that the students are in control and deliver in a more formal way what their group has negotiated. There is information about the experiment's design so the audience understands to a certain degree what happens in the experiment but there is also some explanation required about why they have made certain decisions.

It is unlikely, however, that the students provide as much information and reasoning as is desired by the teacher so his/her role is to probe what the students think, continually asking why they have chosen this and what would happen if a certain condition existed. This models for the students what kind of thinking is possible.

It is also at this point that the teacher can model and otherwise scaffold the technical language necessary to develop the scientific concepts intended.

Figure 19: Students take on the responsibility to present their thinking to the class and answer questions

Apart from the teacher taking on another role in the class, the above context also demands that the students understand their new roles. The fact that each group presents on a different experiment means that the other students listen to the presentation. If the students were required to take notes on what the students present in order to complete a task, then it would mean that they would listen even more attentively and be more likely to ask questions of their peers. If each group were to present on the same experiment, it is more probable that they will not listen because the task does not require it.

This discussion of one lesson near or at the end of a unit of work shows that there can be planned meso-scaffolding as the teacher designs steps 1 to 3 and that there can be contingent meso-scaffolding as the variables in interactions in each of the steps can be shifted so that students can be challenged moderately.

Register shifts in a biology class

In this section, data from a biology lesson offer opportunities to discuss register shifts and accompanying language choices and thereby exemplify what happens when there are moves back and forth along the register continuum. Analyses of the transcripts allow us to better understand what each situation affords the students in terms of language use and whether the activities and the sequence of those activities are actually achieving their intended purpose.

Each transcript is first analysed according to the three register variables and then the implications of the patterns of language are discussed.

The transcripts are extracts from a lesson on enzymes with students 15 years of age. The class was involved in a group activity that required them to work with cardboard cut-outs representing examples of the lock-and-key hypothesis for how enzymes work (Fig. 20). Each group, made up of three to four students, had different enzyme-substrate complexes and they needed to fit together the pieces that represented the enzyme molecule, the substrate molecule(s) and the product molecule(s). Towards the end of the lesson, each group was asked to present their work to the rest of the class, who were at that stage standing around the teacher's bench at the front of the classroom.

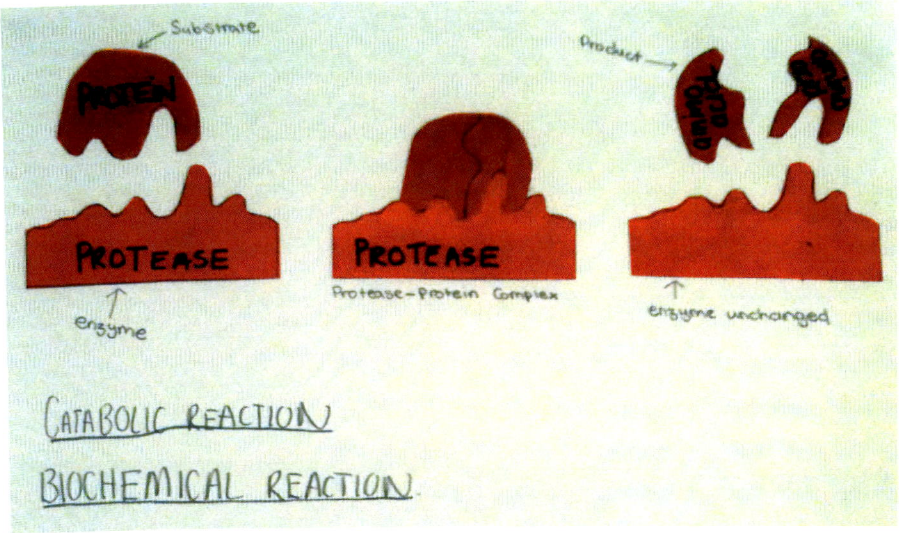

Figure 20: The final arrangement of cardboard cut-outs representing the lock-and-key hypothesis.

Context 1: Students in small group work

Early in the lesson, the teacher came to the students' bench, reiterated and clarified the task for them and then left them on their own. This transcript shows the students working together to complete the task.

Figure 21 (right): Students as a small group collaborating on a task with a set of cut-outs.

Text 21

S2:	Do the arrows go in towards the enzyme?
S3:	Is that how you spell it?
S1:	Yeah. ... So then that and the arrows go ...
S2:	... Wait, do we go like that or...?
S3:	Yeah, you go [points with her hand]
S1:	[sarcastic] No, you go like up and down and....
S3	...and just go around like that [points again]

Field The few terms are concrete and everyday except for enzyme.

Tenor Their roles and relationships are as equal and active participants in the activity. They can command or question each other and are allowed to be sarcastic.

Mode They are working face-to-face at their bench, moving the cut-outs, labelling and talking at the same time. Most of the meanings are understood from being in the context (through the use of pronouns: you, it, that)

In terms of people, place and time: there are few people, the space between them is minimal, and the talk is around things happening there and then.

Context 2: Teacher guiding students in small groups

The students are still at their benches as in Context 1 but the teacher has chosen to come into this group once they had decided how the cut-outs would be arranged. This means that her concern is not about how to do the task but what the outcomes were.

Figure 22 (right): Students consolidating and confirming understanding through teacher scaffolding.

Text 22

T1:	So, can you identify the enzyme? Which one's the enzyme?
S3:	Lipase
T1:	Lipase. Right. Which one is it in the diagram?
S1:	Is it the dark one?
T:	Yep, that's correct. OK, and your substrate?
S1:	Lipid
T1:	Lipid. Where's the lipid there?
S1:	This one. No, this one
S3:	We don't have any
T1:	Yes you have. There's your lipid. What have you actually formed there?
S1:	It's the lock and key so they fit
T1:	Yeah
S2:	(not discernible)
T1:	What do you call that specifically? ...
S3:	...We call that
T1:	...where they've locked in together, what do you call that?
S3:	...the lipase-lipid complex
T1:	Well done. And what's a general term we use for that?
S3:	substrate complex
T3:	No. Enzyme...
S3:	Enzyme-substrate complex
T1:	Excellent. And what have you formed there?
S3:	Lipase and fatty acid [complex?] and glycerol
T1:	Well done. Has the actual enzyme changed?
S1&S3:	No
T1:	No. That's a really important thing about enzymes, isn't it? All right, so glue it down and label it

Field A series of technical terms uttered by the students and teacher: enzyme, lipase, lipid, lock and key, enzyme-substrate complex. The other terms are not concerned with enzymes but about the students' understanding of the technical meanings (identify, correct, formed, call, changed...).

Tenor The students' roles are as active participants and their relationships are equal but they are led by the teacher, who has expertise and power and, because of that, is afforded the right to ask questions to check understanding and evaluate their contributions, and then give instructions.

Mode They are working face-to-face at their benches and the cut-out images are in front of them but they are not moving the pieces, although they can lift a piece when it is mentioned. Rather, they are observing what they have already done and reflecting on it. There is some pronoun use (it, there, this, we, you, that).

In terms of people, place and time: there are still few people but the inclusion of an extra person (the teacher) causes the shift; they are all next to each other and the talk is around immediate things, although the time has shifted slightly because they are now talking about their results.

Context 3: Student groups presenting to the class

Towards the end of the lesson, each group of students is required to go to the front of the class, post their arrangements on the board and share the responsibility for presenting. Text 23 came before Text 24 in terms of the order of the presentations.

Figure 23 (right): A student group presenting their understanding to the whole class.

Text 23

S1: This chemical reaction is a catabolic reaction as it broke down the substrate. It's a biochemical reaction, too.

S2: Our enzyme is cellulase.

S3:	Our substrate is cellulose.
S1:	So, in the reaction, the cellulase and the cellulose become the cellulase–cellulose substrate, which was the enzyme-substrate complex.
S4:	And the product of our reaction was glucose and the enzyme remained unchanged.

Text 24

S1:	Our ... was a catabolic reaction. Our substrate was lactose and our enzyme was lactase.
S2:	As you can see, the enzyme-substrate complex, which is a lactase-lactose complex, is shown as a binding and provides the active site and it produces the products. Oh, it breaks down the products of the disaccharide lactose into the lactose and glucose.
T1:	Well done, girls.
T2:	So what was your enzyme again?
SS-T2:	Lactase!

Field Almost all the content words are technical or, at least, specialised.

Tenor The students are now taking on expert roles and informing the class about their results. A teacher is the only one to ask a question. At the end of Text 24, the teacher evaluates the students' contribution and asks a confirming question.

Mode The students are at the front of the class, able to face their audience although the high challenge of the context results in them facing mainly the other group members rather than the whole class. Each student can refer to their group's cut-outs to inform what they say. The communication is still spoken but the cut-out images are placed on the whiteboard for all to see. However, even though the speakers are close to the cut-outs and can point to them and the cut-outs can be seen by everyone, some students may not be close enough to read the labels.

In terms of people, place and time: the number of people the group is presenting to is now the whole class, the speakers are close to each other but further from the listeners, and, although the talk is about immediate things, it represents meanings that can be generalised.

Context 4: Teacher asking the class questions at the end of the lesson

In this context, the teacher comes to the front of the class after all the students have presented and places herself next to the board with all the posters on it and goes through a final process of questions and answers to confirm the students' understanding.

Text 25

T1:	Just one more thing. When you look at that, the differences, is there a difference? We've said (there are) a lot of similarities. Is there anything...
S:	different shape
T1:	... different shape? Where in particular are the shapes different?
S:	... at the lock and key
S:	... at the active site
T1:	at the active site, yeah. So the active site is different between each of them so that brings up the whole issue that, you know that... Could you get protease and try to react it with cellulose?
SS:	No
T1:	Could I react cellulose with lactose?
SS:	No
T1:	... It's pretty specific, isn't it? That active site is specific for a particular substrate. Fair enough? Good? Yeah?

Field Some of the lexis is technical but most of the words construe non-technical meanings.

Tenor The students' roles are now as informed co-contributors. The teacher is still in power and so asks questions but the questions are confirming the students' knowledge rather than building it up from scratch.

Mode The students are still positioned close to the board but the teacher is at the board now. She refers to all the visuals of the enzyme-substrate complexes on the board and is not asking questions about any specific visual.

In terms of people, place and time: the number of people is still at the maximum for the class, the speaker and listeners are still separated by some distance, and the talk is more about meanings that can be generalised.

Figure 24 shows what we would expect if these four contexts were located on the register continuum. Note that Context 4 shifts back as it allows the teacher to interact in a more spoken way with the class but this is now when they have shown they are more knowledgeable about the lock-and-key hypothesis.

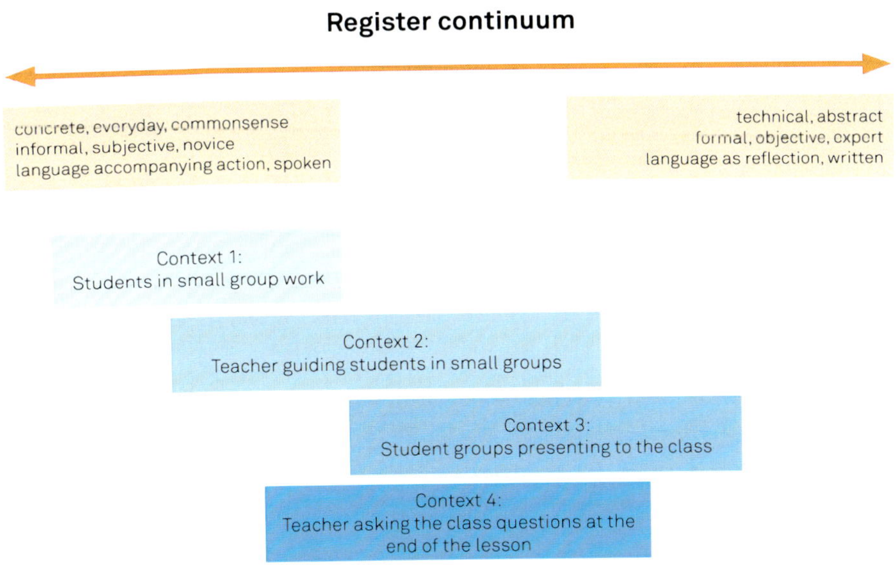

Figure 24: Meso-scaffolding achieved through register shifts in phases of a lesson

What is important in the macro- and meso-scaffolding is that the activities are sequenced and the nature of the activities is changed so that students are challenged but supported as they engage in learning. The analyses of the three variables of people, place and time illustrates how the nature of the activities are changed. For many students, asking them to go from Context 1 to 3 is a considerable jump. If the teacher is not able to go to every group in the class, then they would be even more dependent on the teacher's instructions prior to their presentations. Also, if the teacher is confident that the first group chosen to present (Text 23) would do it well, then their presentation could act as a model for the other groups. The teacher could have made a point of speaking to the group during Context 2. In summary, the choices made in a lesson are so that the students are challenged but not placed in a position where they would likely fail.

The lesson on enzymes that has been used to illustrate how context varies and, therefore, how language varies, has had the students physically engaged in an activity. Yet, they were not experimenting or carrying out an investigation, which were the genres for 'doing' science given in Figure 1. So this highlights an important point to make about how one thinks about the nature of the activities teachers can design for their classes. It is useful for classroom work to start from somewhere on the left of the register continuum and then move to the right because it allows for the students to be scaffolded into learning the intended technical and abstract meanings. 'Doing' science might be understood as doing experiments but much of science cannot be 'done' in the school laboratory. This could be because it is too macro (such as anything to do with the universe) or too micro (such as at the molecular or atomic level) or too dangerous (such as radioactivity but also strong acids and bases, or human organs) or too expensive (such as using any precious metals).

Therefore, how do teachers make the teaching and learning of these scientific fields engaging? A principal way is by providing multiple access points to the meaning by exploiting all the multisemiotic resources available. For phenomena that are not possible to access through experiments, then providing simulations and animated representations of the scientific phenomena are excellent ways. But it is still very often observing someone else's actions. To make the students physically active, teachers need to consider how they can get them to manipulate the knowledge. The activity on enzymes, where the students had the component parts, as cut-outs, to work with the lock-and-key hypothesis, is one example. Another way is to make texts themselves the objects of discussion and manipulation by, for example, engaging students in analysing texts in the way that was shown with macrogeneric texts and visuals in texts.

Another consequence of not being able to do experiments on all the scientific knowledge covered in school science is the crucial need to develop high literacy levels since students are now dependent on the print and visual texts constructed from the research of professional scientists. If we define literacy as being the capacity to make meaning bi-directionally — to make sense of someone else's constructed meanings and also to construct meanings for someone else to understand in the ways intended — then students need to be good readers, viewers and writers. Understanding how texts are constructed in patterned ways is invaluable, therefore, in becoming a good reader, viewer and writer just as looking for patterns is invaluable in becoming a good scientist. The knowledge and the pedagogical tools that are presented in this book are intended to build the meta-understanding of the patterned ways of meaning in science.

Writing plays an important role in school science. Writing science texts, for example, unlike filling-in-the-gaps activities, or giving one-word or short-phrase answers, or answering multiple choice questions, requires planning and a series of decisions. This concurs with van Lier's (2004) assertion that working alone, which is what independent writing entails, ought to be considered a contributing element to scaffolding. If we go back to the kinds of questions asked about the different sample genres given, we can see that a writer would need to make a number of decisions when writing the texts. Some of the many questions could be:

- Is the content in the right order?
- Have I defined these terms correctly?
- Is this statement a 'fact' or not?
- What is the cause (or consequence) of this phenomenon?
- What did I really observe and can I be sure it was caused by that variable?
- Would someone else be able to understand my explanation?
- Can I give an analogy?

These questions and the decisions made are what could become visible and audible in the modelling and deconstruction stages of the cycle of teaching and learning, which is what will be addressed in the next section, after micro-scaffolding.

Micro-scaffolding

Micro-scaffolding is contingent scaffolding — happening when it is possible or necessary — and we will consider it in the phase of the biology lesson when the teacher is interacting with a group that has completed their task of arranging their cut-outs (Text 22). Figure 25 presents an analysis of the kind of scaffolding that is present in the interaction.

		Micro-scaffolding strategies
T1:	So, can you identify the enzyme? Which one's the enzyme?	*Rephrases previous question more simply*
S3:	Lipase	
T1:	Lipase. Right. Which one is it in the diagram?	*Repeats student's response, evaluates and asks a specific question of location*
S1:	Is it the dark one?	
T:	Yep, that's correct. OK, and your substrate?	
S1:	Lipid	
T1:	Lipid. Where's the lipid there?	*Repeats student's response, and asks a more specific question of location*
S1:	This one. No, this one	
S3:	We don't have any	
T1:	Yes you have. There's your lipid. What have you actually formed there?	*Points to the correct answer at the same time as uttering it*
S1:	It's the lock and key so they fit	
T1:	Yeah	
S2:	(not discernible)	
T1:	What do you call that specifically? ...	*Changes original question ('...actually formed there?') to a less ambiguous one ('...call that specifically?')*
S3:	...We call that	
T1:	...where they've locked in together, what do you call that?	*Affirms that their lock and key answer was not wrong by using 'locked in together' but points and pushes for a more specific answer*
S3:	...the lipase-lipid complex	
T1:	Well done. And what's a general term we use for that?	*Evaluates positively and then pushes them to a generalised term*
S3:	substrate complex	
T3:	No. Enzyme...	*Offers the beginning of the full term and through intonation indicates that they are able to finish it*
S3:	Enzyme-substrate complex	
T1:	Excellent. And what have you formed there?	*Evaluates positively and moves to the next phase in the reaction*

S3:	Lipase and fatty acid [complex?] and glycerol	
T1:	Well done. Has the actual enzyme changed?	*Evaluates positively and moves to the component of the reaction that doesn't change*
S1 & S3:	No	
T1:	No. That's a really important thing about enzymes, isn't it? All right, so glue it down and label it	*Evaluates positively by confirming with a tagged clause the importance of their knowledge*

Figure 25: Micro-scaffolding of a small group of students by the teacher

Not all scaffolding strategies are of equal value or strength and they can also be considered on a cline (e.g. Dansie 2001). Some of the micro-scaffolding strategies used by the teacher in this text are weaker than others but what is clear from the analysis is that a significant benefit of the kind of interaction the teacher and students are engaged in is providing opportunities for the students to say aloud the technical meanings. The list of technical terms the students utter in this very short interaction with the expert teacher is lipid, lock and key, lipase-lipid complex, substrate complex, enzyme-substrate complex, lipase and fatty acid [complex?] and glycerol. In other words, most, if not all, of the technical terms necessary to talk about this reaction have been spoken aloud and correctly by the students. Later, when the students present to the whole class, they are required to say these very terms, and not in a dialogue as here, so this interaction is an opportunity to consolidate and rehearse, or recycle, the knowledge in its technical construction. The quality of the presentations would suggest that the micro-scaffolding and the hands-on activity successfully prepared them. The unanswered question for this class is whether the teacher has consciously gone to this group because she was aware, based on her experiences, that this group needed stronger scaffolding for the presentations than other groups in the class.

Cycles of teaching and learning

In this section, we bring together the macro-, meso- and micro-scaffolding into a holistic approach through cycles of teaching and learning. The initial research into a genre-based pedagogy produced a cycle of teaching and learning about writing (Callaghan and Rothery 1988). Various versions of the cycle have been developed (Rothery 1996, Martin 1999, Custance, Dare & Polias 2011, Polias & Forey (2016), Forey & Polias (forthcoming)) and the version here is a further extension. An important point to make at the outset is that the teaching and learning cycle presented here is not only concerned with writing, it encompasses various processes of teaching and learning.

Figure 26 illustrates the teaching and learning cycle in which there are four stages: setting the context, modelling and deconstruction, guided (or joint) construction and independent construction. It describes what each of these stages might entail and what responsibility the teacher and students have as the lessons go around the cycle. Within the cycle, the teacher is gradually handing over the responsibility for the learning and the students are, similarly, gradually taking over the responsibility for the learning. All the while, there is development of the knowledge and, as the class goes through the stages, there is ongoing assessment of the success of the learning. As the class goes through cycle after cycle, they are learning the curriculum.

The guided construction stage in the cycle is typically the stage in which micro-scaffolding is most evident. The term, joint construction, is used by many educators rather than guided construction but there is the risk that teachers will accept that having students doing any group work is part of micro-scaffolding; there is no guarantee that any challenging work is occurring simply because students are in a group. Therefore, as a way of stressing the importance of guidance by a knowledgeable or informed other, guided construction is being used here.

A variety of options in this stage but the teacher is usually in control with the students providing some kind of input

1. Setting the context

- Starting out by presenting what is to be learned and the aims.
- Discussing current knowledge and questions that may still need to be answered.
- Activities for exploring ways of understanding are guided by the teacher.

Student responsibility

4. Independent construction

The teacher is confident the students have been suitably prepared by the previous three stages in the cycle and so students now complete the final (assessable) task by themselves with assistance provided if necessary. And then the cycles continue.

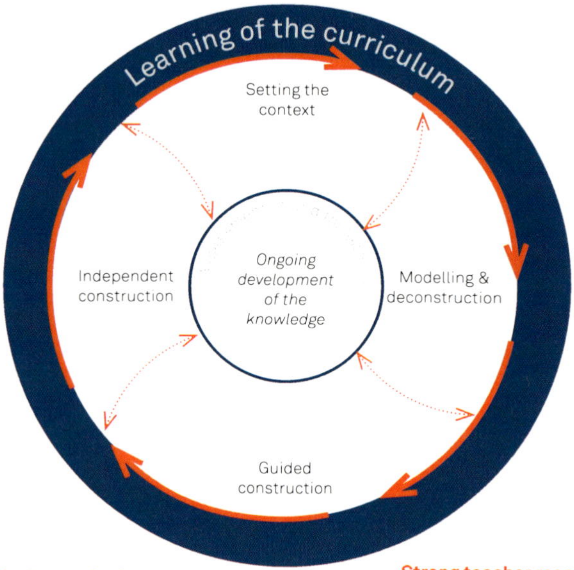

Responsibility shifts increasingly from the teacher to the students

3. Guided construction

The teacher is now moving on to something more challenging for the students but is guiding them through the process by various micro- and meso-scaffolding means, eg:

- posing probing questions that scaffold the students
- referring back to the modelling and deconstruction activities and supporting the students to make visible and audible their decision-making processes
- providing multiple ways of accessing the meanings.

Strong teacher responsibility

2. Modelling & deconstruction

- Showing students how to do something or explain something, presenting all the parts and modelling each of those.
- Making sure students are able to access again what the teacher has presented, either because the meanings have been written down and/or visuals have been provided.
- Making visible and audible the decision-making processes.
- Breaking down the learning into 'manageable bits'.

Figure 26: A cycle of teaching and learning incorporating degrees of responsibility

Although the cycle was theorised for schooling contexts, a similar cycle is used and has been used in everyday life when dealing with, for example, dangerous or very expensive activities. Dealing with these kinds of activities highlights most clearly the process of teaching and learning in a cycle. In school, for example, a laboratory experiment with dangerous chemicals would have the teacher going very carefully through the four stages of the teaching and learning cycle, making sure before they get to the last stage that the students are very well prepared before carrying out an activity independently. The irony is that this is seen only as a matter of safety rather than a matter of learning. Too often, students are asked to go from the teacher showing them something to them being able to go and do it by themselves. The risk of failure or moderate success is heightened and, with this, comes the risk of an affective response by the students, such as a lack of motivation to continue to be interested in their learning.

Rothery (1996) discussed the possibility of retracing steps in the cycle but the original diagram did not highlight that aspect. Figure 27 shows what it might look like for a unit of work made up of multiple lessons. It sets out a unit of work on teaching students how to write a Laboratory Report and illustrates how the model can incorporate smaller teaching and learning cycles, or mini-cycles (blue, dashed circles), of varying time length. In this way, we can show the complexities of teaching and learning in a classroom. The large cycle (orange, dashed circle) can represent the processes in a single lesson but, more commonly, can represent multiple lessons.

A mini-cycle may be viewed as something that is decided at a specific moment in the lesson to respond to a need that was not planned for. However, it is more likely that the more planned a major cycle is, the more the mini-cycles are planned, too. The sequencing of the large cycle and mini-cycles provides the macro-scaffolds, while the events within the mini-cycles afford the teacher and students all the opportunities for meso- and micro-scaffolding. Polias and Forey (2016) provide a fuller description of the possible cycles of teaching and learning, and Christie (1997, 1998) explains cycles of teaching and learning activities as curriculum genres and curriculum macrogenres.

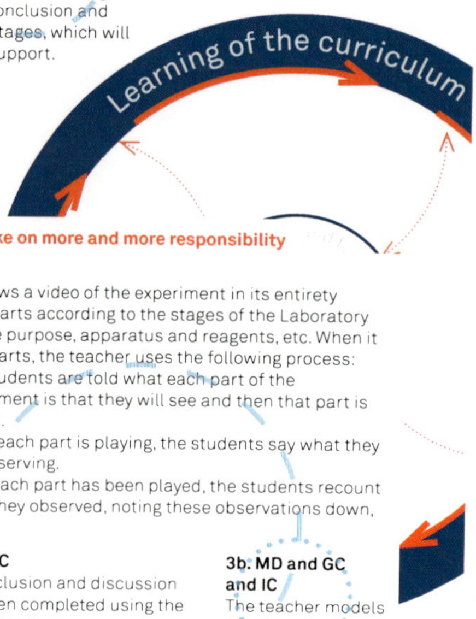

ONGOING CYCLES

IC (and iterations of SC, MD, GC and IC)
In another teaching cycle and, of course, another experiment, the teacher asks the students to complete independently all the stages except the conclusion and discussion stages, which will need more support.

Teacher and students share responsibility

1. Setting the context (SC)
Teacher and students recap different chemical testing methods and then focus on how to test the presence of calcium and carbonate in limestone.

Teacher has strong responsibility initially with some student input later

2a. Modelling & deconstruction (MD)
Teacher hands out 2 model texts to the class and uses these models to show the students the structure of a chemistry Laboratory Report by focusing on the questions that need to be answered by each part of the text.

While the teacher is talking, the students write in their worksheets, alongside each stage, its function and what is expected in that stage.

2b. Guided construction (GC)
Using a new Laboratory Report that is in jumbled order and having turned over their completed worksheets, the teacher asks the students questions in order to put the stages in the right order, making sure the students say clearly the stages' names and what the function of each stage is.

2c. Independent construction (IC)
The class will be focusing on a new but closely related experiment for which they will be writing a Laboratory Report. Before doing that, though, the students write up the stage headings of the Laboratory Report in their worksheets.

Students take on more and more responsibility

3a. SC
The class views a video of the experiment in its entirety and then in parts according to the stages of the Laboratory Report, ie the purpose, apparatus and reagents, etc. When it is shown in parts, the teacher uses the following process:

- The students are told what each part of the experiment is that they will see and then that part is played.
- While each part is playing, the students say what they are observing.
- After each part has been played, the students recount what they observed, noting these observations down, too.

3b. MD and GC and IC
The teacher models how to write the first observation statement, guides the students in writing the next one or two and then the students independently write the remaining observations.

3c. MD and GC
Both the conclusion and discussion stages are then completed using the following process:

- The teacher and students use the 2 model texts to identify the language features of the conclusion and discussion stages.
- The teacher then models an example of how they can write a conclusion (and a discussion).
- The teacher guides the students in writing the beginning sentence of those two stages.
- Then the students complete the remaining part of each stage.

Figure 27: A unit of work in chemistry on teaching students how to write a Laboratory Report

Figure 27 shows how the apparent modelling and deconstruction stage in the major cycle becomes a mini-cycle itself because the teacher has decided that modelling and deconstructing a Laboratory Report could not be done by 'showing and telling' but by requiring the students to be more active in the process. In the second major stage, where the students are gradually being handed the responsibility, the second phase of that mini-cycle is again demanding that the class is involved in another mini-cycle — a mini-cycle within a mini-cycle. This was determined by the teacher as necessary because teaching the students how to write the discussion and conclusion stages of the Laboratory Report was going to require some careful scaffolding. In fact, the discussion and conclusion stages are found to be so difficult for many students that this process needs to be followed carefully and repeated a number of times and even over a number of years; hence, the last mini-cycle in Figure 27, titled 'ongoing cycles'.

The chemistry content (field) of the two Laboratory Reports used in the modelling and deconstruction stage needed to be familiar to the students so that the focus was on the writing of the Laboratory Report. Also, the questions that would be asked in these activities had to be able to be answered by the students because the answers were within their 'reach'. For the students, the answers were in front of them and not in some imagined or hoped for experience in their reading or practice. That is why two texts were used to compare. It is much easier to ask a student to find the generic patterns in a text if they are asked what the two texts have in common than to find the features of a single text. This follows the principles of science, where scientists do not look at a phenomenon in isolation but look to establish its features by finding similarities and differences with other phenomena.

Figure 27 illustrates the benefits in thinking of genre as a socio-cultural activity. Teachers and students do not arrive at a final, assessable text in one move. There are units of work planned and lessons planned and, as we can see in the cycles of teaching and learning in Figure 27, there is a range of activities and decisions made and formative texts constructed before the final assessable text is constructed. What is happening in these cycles is that the genre is being enacted. The enactment of any genre in schooling contexts needs to include the decisions and activities that comprise the mini-cycles leading up to the point where a teacher can say that it is the end point, where certain configurations of meanings that were the goal of the unit of work have been reached. This is an elaborate view of genre that acknowledges that all the activities that a class undertakes has a role to play in the construction of the generic meanings. That is why the word enacting is used. The meanings come into being through these activities. Acknowledging that all the formative activities have a role to play in the construction of the generic meanings is why educators need to consider carefully how they teach what they teach and make sure as much as possible that there is pedagogical resonance (Polias 2010) in their classrooms.

Language resources for 'doing' science

"The evolution of science was, we would maintain, the evolution of scientific grammar…the grammatical resources of the natural languages by which science came to be construed…The evolution of science was the evolution of scientific thought. But thought…is construed in language; and the powerhouse of a language is its grammar."
Halliday (1993)

In other words, the evolution of science is the evolution of scientific thought is the evolution of scientific grammar is the evolution of science is … and the evolution continues. With that as our departure point, we embark on the exploration of language patterns. The language of the macro-scaffold given in Figure 15 can now be looked at more carefully so that the patterns that we have been talking about are identified and start to show some of their potential.

The functional model of language, as presented in Figure 14, shows a direct link between each of the register variables (field, tenor and mode) and the internal functions of language:

- field and the language for expressing content (representing experience) and logic
- tenor and the language for interacting with others
- mode and the language of orientation, organisation and flow.

The term 'internal functions' is typically used to refer to all the systems that work inside a mechanism or organism to allow the mechanism or organism to work; that is, to carry out its external function. So, for a human body, there are many internal systems that all work together to allow the body to carry out its external functions, such as to do work or move from place to place or think or eat or reproduce. Language can be seen as having such systems that work together to allow us to use language for our purposes. In other words, for each language function, there are patterns of internal systems that educators would be interested in because it is these patterns that are the keys to constructing and giving access to scientific knowledge.

Let us reiterate the argument for why science teachers should look at language more closely. If the register continuum shows how education moves students to the right along the continuum, then the question arises as to which resources are used to make that happen. If we accept that language is our primary resource as humans for making meaning, then it is the development of language resources that allow us to make the increasingly technical and abstract meanings that are necessary to be apprenticed into science. The argument being put forward here is that a pedagogy that is shaped by understanding how this happens is a pedagogy that is more likely to scaffold all students to maximise their learning. The aspects of language taken up in this book are the ones that over twenty years of working in this way with science teachers have shown to be the most pertinent for them.

Patterns of language for representing experience

The first system examined here is the system that represents experience or, more simply put, expresses content. The system is made up of three groupings, each of which answers certain questions about our experience. Figure 28 shows these groupings using the method stage of an Experiment because the grammar is easier to analyse but also because it is the first genre in the macro-scaffold given in Figure 15.

Processes	Participants	Circumstances
Processes tell us what is going on. In the method stage of Experiments, the processes construe actions, so we can ask, e.g.: "What do we have to do?"	Participants tell us who or what is participating in the process. If the process is an action, we ask who does the action or who or what the action is done to. In this text, we ask, e.g.: "What do we have to take?", "What do we have to boil?"	Circumstances tell us something about the action itself, eg the manner or time or place of the action. We can ask in this text, e.g.: "Where do we boil it?"

	Take a small green leaf from a healthy plant.
	Boil some water in a beaker
and	then turn down the Bunsen flame.
	Use forceps
	to dip the leaf into the boiling water for about one minute.
	Take out the leaf
and	place it at the bottom of a large test tube —
	push it to the bottom with a glass rod.
	Put on your goggles
and	then pour enough ethanol to cover the leaf.

Patterns of language

The text analysis is arranged so that a new clause starts on a new line (a clause is a chunk of meaning built around a process.) In the discussion of the nominal group, it will be seen that the clause 'to cover the leaf' is functioning inside the nominal group to qualify 'ethanol'.

The typical pattern in the method stage of an Experiment is for the processes of action to be at the front in English in order to orientate the meanings to the actions required. Occasionally, elements of time or manner come at the front.

The participants in the action are concrete (typically the materials or apparatus) and not very technical.

The circumstances around action processes are typically of time, place and manner.

Figure 28: Functional groupings that express content

Each grouping can be identified using three colours and these three — green for processes, red for participants, and blue for circumstances — are now used widely in educational contexts (Custance, Dare and Polias 2011). The labels for the functional groupings — process, participant and circumstance — are important, as any technical term is important, but it is just as important for teachers and students to be concerned with the questions that realise the functions. The significance of these questions is that, because they are concerned with content rather than linguistic labels such as subject and object, these are the typical kinds of questions a teacher of science would ask anyway. What we are able to do with the systemic-functional model of language is point to those language elements that work together to realise those functions.

Figure 29 shows the typical choices when recounting the method of an Experiment. To move from the Experiment (the text of instructions) to the Procedural Recount (the text of recounted actions) requires a change in the grammar from the grammar of direct instructions (e.g. 'Push it.') to the grammar typical of statements (e.g. 'I pushed it.') Additionally, Figure 29 also provides an example where the orientation is to the scientist and an example with the orientation to the 'science'. In the former, the voice is the active voice and in the latter it is referred to as the passive voice and additional grammatical elements to construct it are needed (see Fig. 47). As we saw when discussing Laboratory Reports and Investigations, either of these two orientations is possible, although Investigations appear to demand a greater degree of orientation to the scientist. This is due to Investigations requiring the student to take on the responsibility for deciding which processes to carry out in the Investigation.

Procedural Recount

Orientation to the scientist

We took a small green leaf from a healthy plant,
boiled some water in a beaker
and then turned down the Bunsen flame.
We used forceps
to dip the leaf into the boiling water for about one minute.

Orientation to the 'science'

The leaf was taken out
and placed at the bottom of a large test tube.
It was pushed to the bottom with a glass rod.
Goggles were put on
and then enough ethanol to cover the leaf was poured over it.

Patterns of language

The lexical resources (content words) of these two texts are the same as those of the Experiment. What has changed, though, is the grammar: these two texts are not instructing but making statements in the past tense. That typically involves two participants around the process: the do-er of the action and the receiver of the action, the done-to.

Comparing these texts, we can see that both texts are in the past tense but they are oriented to different things: the first is to the humans, the scientists ('we'), while the second is to the non-humans or what could be called the science (e.g. 'the leaf'). However, having the done-to at the front requires some additional work in the verbal group that expresses the process—the construction of the passive voice ('was poured').

Figure 29: Patterns in a Procedural Recount with alternative orientations

The next genre in the macro-scaffold in Figure 15 is the Sequential Explanation with human agency. Explanations, both temporal and non-temporal, make generalised meanings and this example is in reaction to a question such as: "How does one test for starch?" Or it can be expressed as "How is the process carried out?" If we are not interested in the testing, in other words, not interested in any human involvement in the explanation, then the question of interest would more likely be "How is starch formed by plants?", which is the next genre in the macro-scaffold, Sequential Explanation without human agency.

Now we see the language choices in the macro-scaffold more clearly (Fig. 30) and we can see how big the shifts are along the register continuum. Between the instructions in the first text example and the recounting in the second text example, there is a minor shift and, therefore, one that should be easily manageable by the students. The shift to the Explanation with human agency is slightly larger. The change in tense might look innocuous but it is the generalised meanings that create a hurdle for the students. The students feel more comfortable with actions they are involved in. To express actions that other scientists, collectively, carry out is harder. And the shift to the Explanation without human agency is the hardest of the four given in this macro-scaffold since the meanings are not necessarily in the students' experiences but in the experiences of professional scientists.

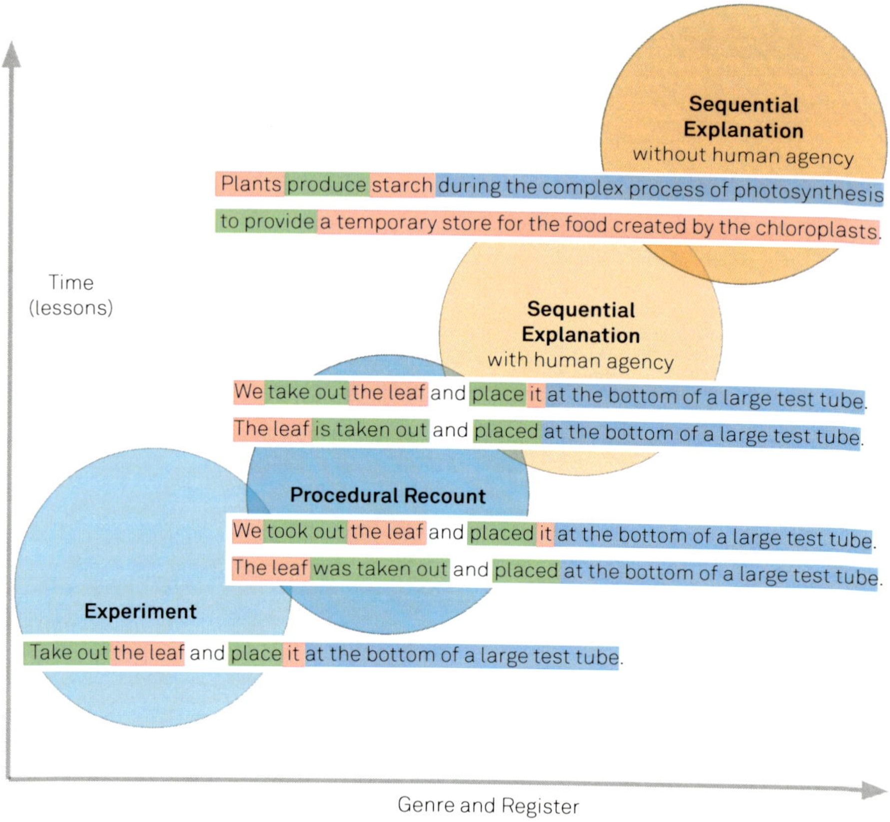

Figure 30: Changing patterns of language in a sample macro-scaffold

Constructing technicality and abstraction

The language choices in the final Sequential Explanation example from Figure 30 illustrate the resources that are available to us to make technical and abstract meanings. If we look at the processes (in green), we can see that there is not much potential for increasing technicality. It might be possible to say that 'produce' and 'provide' are slightly more abstract than 'took out' and 'place' and we might point to examples such as 'synthesise' and 'oxidise' but, if we think about all the kinds of technical meanings science is comprised of, then we conclude that something other than the processes is doing most of the work. We see that the participants in the processes have the potential to be greatly expanded, e.g. 'a temporary store for the food created by the chloroplasts'. Also, there is something in the circumstances (in blue) that similarly can be expanded, e.g. 'the complex process of photosynthesis'.

However, it is possible to add further information in other ways. Let us compare the two major ways of adding information — we can label these two ways as 'adding information loosely' and 'adding information tightly'. We can explore these two major ways by using answers to the question: "Which renewable energy sources are suitable for generating electricity in Hong Kong and why?"

Adding information loosely

	Hong Kong has a couple of possible sources of renewable energy
and	it'd be good
so	we don't have to use fossil fuels.
	One energy source is the sun
and	the other is the wind
because	Hong Kong gets a lot of sunshine
and	it is quite windy.

To add information loosely, clauses are strung together with complex logic, such as addition and cause, using one of the major language resources available to do this, conjunctions. In the above, we have 3 clauses in the first sentence and four clauses in the second. There are only about 18 lexical items (content words) over a total of 7 clauses for a density of about 2.6 lexical items per clause. In other words, the average number of content words in each of the clauses making up this short text is 2.6. That lexical density is quite easy for a listener to process and is typical of spoken language.

Adding information tightly

The two most suitable renewable energy sources for Hong Kong are the sun and wind because of its plentiful sunshine and wind.

To add information tightly, we do not simply string clauses together but, instead, we pack in the information by expanding nominal groups. In the above sentence, we have a single clause and 11 lexical items for a lexical density of 11, which is typical of highly written texts. The main difference between the two is that, to move from a lexical density of 2.6 content words per clause to 11 content words per clause, the writer needs to exploit the potential the nominal group offers. So, because writing offers much more time to plan carefully what is chosen in the language and the arrangement of those choices, the option to expand the nominal group is readily taken up.

Understanding the nominal group

The nominal group, as the resource in the grammar that allows language users to pack in information, can be defined as a group of words that coalesce around a central noun. Figure 31 shows patterns in the nominal group and how it is related to both participants and circumstances. It also shows how we can expand a nominal group from its single core noun.

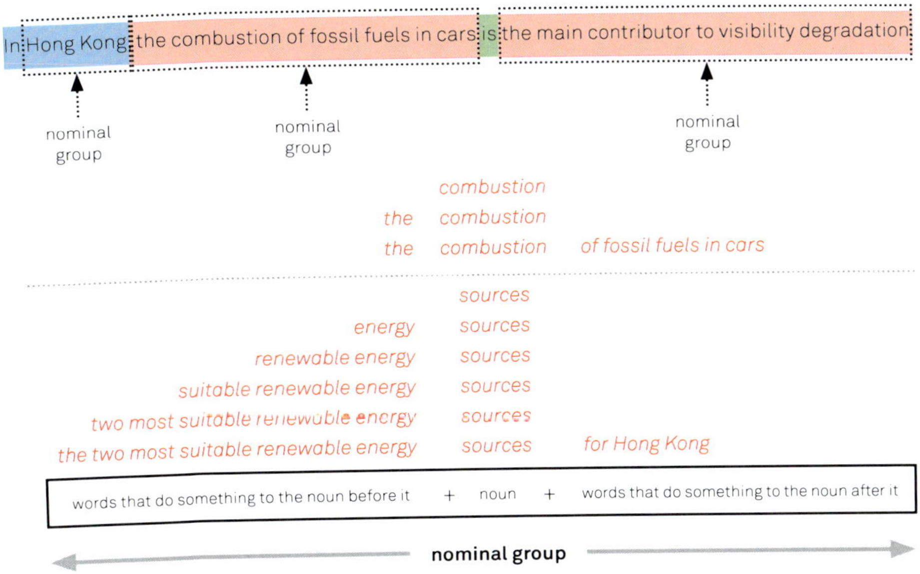

Figure 31: Expanding the nominal group

Science greatly exploits the nominal group and success in making the kinds of technical meanings expected in school science requires developing control of the nominal group.

Let us now examine what potential the nominal group offers us; in other words, what kinds of questions are answered by the elements that make up the nominal group. The nominal group in English has certain, rather strict arrangements (Fig. 32). Note that, as long as we have even a single word, we have a nominal group. For example, 'homo sapiens', 'woman', and 'she' are all examples of nominal groups.

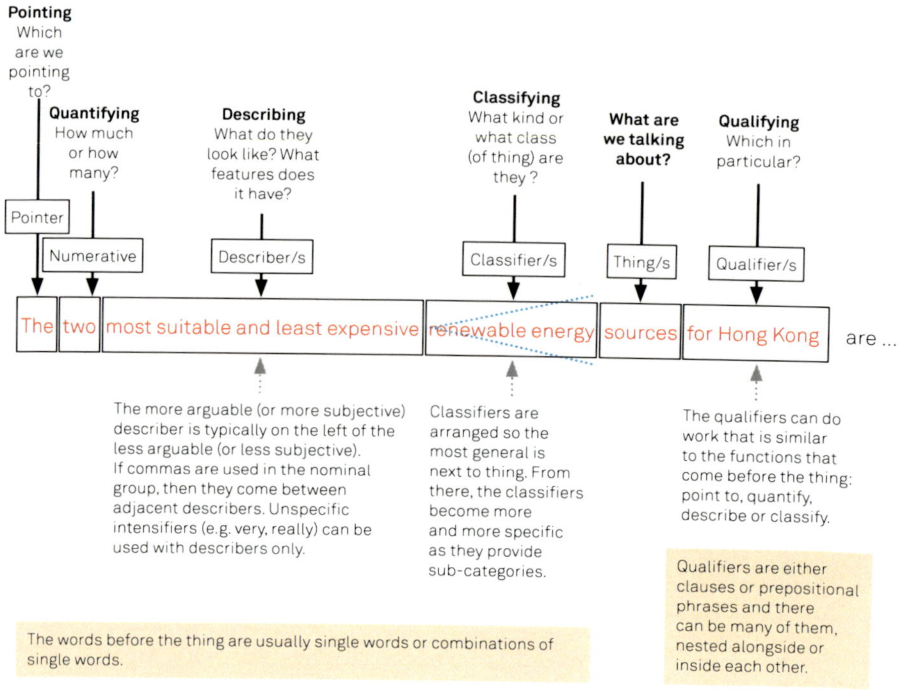

Figure 32: Patterns of meaning in the nominal group

The constituent elements of the nominal group

Thing

The thing (a noun or noun complex) is the central element around which the other meanings are arranged. If you cut away every other word in the group, this word would be the last remaining one. It answers the question: What are we talking about?

Classifiers

To the immediate left of the thing come the words whose function is to classify the thing in a technical way (and hence set up the scientific discipline) by answering questions such as: 'What kind or what class?' An example is classifying momentum as angular momentum, where the word 'angular' is the classifier. There can be any number of classifiers with each one sub-classifying the next. For example, in 'renewable energy sources', energy classifies the source and then renewable classifies the energy.

Describers

To the left of any classifiers come describers, whose function is to present some descriptive feature or characteristic of the thing. Describers present some quality or feature of a thing that does not construct the discipline in the way a classifier does; they are more an individual's representation of the world. For example, 'contaminated' in 'contaminated sample' is simply giving some feature or characteristic of the sample. However, 'white-tailed' in 'white-tailed eagle' is not simply a describing feature of the eagle but a classifying feature. To ensure the difference is noted, uppercase is often used for classifiers, as in 'juvenile White-tailed Eagle'.

Figure 32 outlines some patterns within both the classifiers and the describers. One way to distinguish a describer from a classifier is that describers can be intensified using non-technical or non-specific words such as very, quite, really and incredibly, whereas classifiers cannot. One can say very suitable and incredibly expensive but cannot say very renewable or really energy. Another way is the tone we say these: classifiers, as discipline-constructing elements, are usually expressed in a monotone, no matter how many classifiers we have, while describers, as individual choices, are expressed with changing intonation. This changing intonation pattern in describers is the reason we usually place commas between two adjacent describers. Conversely, the monotone for classifiers is the reason we do not place commas between any classifiers; for example, 'primordial germ cells', 'secondary sexual characteristics', 'kinetic friction force', 'relative atomic mass'.

It is important to note that the function of a word depends on the context. For example, 'secondary' and 'relative' could be classifiers ('secondary sexual characteristics', 'realtive atomic mass') in one context and describers ('It's a secondary issue', 'the relative value of…') in another context.

Numeratives

To the left of the describers comes the element whose function is to measure or quantify the thing in some way. As for the other elements, this could be a single word (two) or it could be a phrase ('a couple of', '4 mg of', 'two litres of').

Pointers

The pointer is on the left of the numerative and its purpose is to point to the thing we are talking about by using words such as 'the', 'those', these', 'our', 'the metal's'. Sometimes numeratives and pointers are indistinguishable, as in 'a'.

Qualifiers

Moving to the right of the thing, we come to the qualifier(s). This is a very complex part of the nominal group in English for a number of reasons. Their complexity comes from the fact that qualifiers are often a combination of prepositional phrases or clauses and because clauses and prepositional phrases contain their own nominal groups, then qualifiers can be very complex with multiple nestings (Fig. 33).

Patterns in nominal groups in scientific texts

Scientific fields are able to be constructed through taking advantage of the potential the nominal group to classify, describe, quantify and qualify — all packed around an entity, the thing. We will now look at extracts from several texts in order to identify patterns across scientific texts and see if certain functional groups are relied on more than others. A range of nominal groups have been selected in the texts to be analysed and Figure 33 sets out their analyses. Those selected have been bolded in the extracts. Not all the nominal groups in each extract have been selected but those that have will suffice in terms of illustrating the tendencies in the patterns in scientific texts.

Extract from a Classification on EM waves

Light waves are ***electromagnetic waves that are visible****, that is, they lie within* ***the human response spectrum****. Our eyes use light so we can see, although very bright light can damage the retina in our eyes. Green plants need light to grow and they, in turn, then provide energy for many things on earth. We use light for many purposes: to make films and videos; and for laser rays used in industry and medicine. It is also used in* ***optical fibre cables*** *for* ***highly efficient telecommunication****.*

Extract from a Sequential Explanation about the processing of copper ore

The cathodes, which are now ***pure copper metal sheets****, are removed from* ***the chemical bath****. These sheets are ready for removal from* ***the stainless steel backing plates. Bundles***

of pure copper sheets *are prepared for export overseas or sale to* ***local manufacturing companies.***

Extract from a Consequential Explanation on the effects of air pollution

Acid rain *is* ***a chemical phenomenon caused by the dissolution of nitrogen oxides and sulphur dioxide in rainwater to form nitric acid and sulphuric acid.*** *The oxides are released during* ***the combustion of fossil fuels by cars, factories and power plants.*** *Acid rain has* ***multiple adverse effects on ecosystems, where plants and soils are degraded, and on humans and property. Irritation of respiratory systems*** *and* ***corrosion of buildings and car bodies*** *are some of the ways acid rain afflicts people.*

Which are we pointing to? **POINTER**	How many or how much? **NUMERATIVE**	What do they look like? What features do they have? **DESCRIBER/S**	What kind or class (of thing) are they? **CLASSIFIER/S**	What are we talking about? **THING/S**	Which thing in particular? **QUALIFIER/S**
			electromagnetic	waves	that are visible
the			human response	spectrum	
			optical fibre	cables	
		highly efficient		telecommunication	
			pure copper metal	sheets	
the			chemical	bath	
the			stainless steel backing	plates	
	bundles of		pure copper	sheets	
			local manufacturing	companies	
			acid	rain	
a			chemical	phenomenon	caused by the dissolution of nitrogen oxides and sulphur dioxide in rainwater to form nitric acid and sulphuric acid
the				combustion	of fossil fuels by cars, factories and power plants
	multiple	adverse		effects	on ecosystems, where plants and soils are degraded, and on humans and property.
				irritation	of respiratory systems
				corrosion	of buildings and car bodies

Figure 33: Analysis of language choices in the nominal groups of scientific texts

There are a number of observations we can make just from these extracts. If we consider the things first, we see that many of them are technical or specialised (waves, sheets, bath) and others are abstract (phenomenon, effects) and others are a combination of the two (spectrum, telecommunication, corrosion). It is not necessary for teachers to be able to distinguish with students between the two but it shows that the actual entity that is talked about can be difficult to pin down.

The other major pattern is that the classifiers are a functional grouping that is dominant with the qualifiers also being important. The describers and others are not significant at all. This would be expected because science is more interested in taxonomising phenomena in the world in technical ways than describing and the resources for doing that in the language are typically with the classifier grouping. That is not to say that there is no measurement or description but there is a tendency across scientific fields for there to be a focus in the nominal group on classifying and qualifying.

The length of some of the qualifiers also stands out. Qualifiers have a sort of 'catch-all' function. As mentioned, the words that come before the thing are often single words or hyphenated words but it may be difficult to think of a single word to express a certain meaning. In that case, a prepositional phrase or a clause or combinations of these might do the work much more easily and effectively. This is often when a qualifier is used. Also, once the thing is known to the reader, it is possible then to qualify the thing in complex ways. We will see in an examination of definitions that they make use of complex qualifiers in defining the technical term.

Applying knowledge of language in the science classroom

Figure 34, which is based on class work of a science teacher, illustrates how an understanding of processes, participants and circumstances and nominal groups is applied in the classroom.

Patterns of questioning

Through questioning, the teacher starts to build up the field of digestion. The questions combine both clause level and group level questions. In Steps 1 and 3, at the clause level, they are about participants, processes and circumstances. In Step 2, the questions are about parts (dotted underlines) of the nominal group that constitute the two participants.

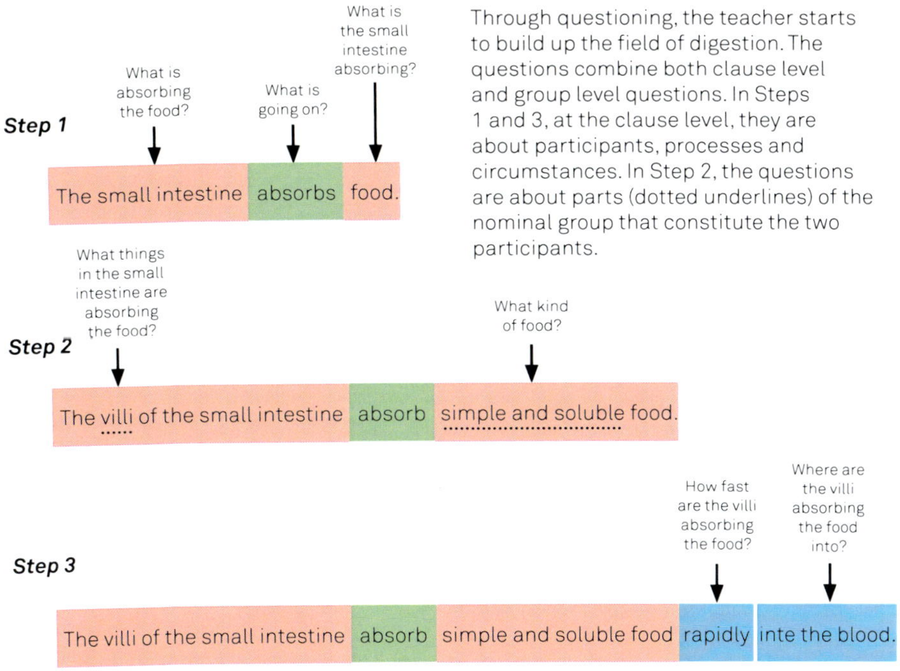

Figure 34: Questions in the classroom informed through patterns of language

Constructing definitions

Definitions play an important role in taking technical perspectives on the everyday world. Their grammatical structure is quite simple because they are set up as an equation — the equal sign in the examples of definitions in Figure 35 shows that they are in essence one and the same thing — on one side is the technical word to be defined, and on the other is the wording that defines the technical word. The equal sign can be worded in many different ways but they are all synonymous with defining or naming. The complexity in definitions is in the nominal group that realises the participant being equated with the technical term and it is the qualifier in the nominal group that is doing a lot of the work. In Figure 35, the thing of the nominal group in the non-technical term has been bolded so that means that everything after the bolded word is the qualifier. Understanding how qualifiers are constructed in nominal groups would help readers and writers of definitions.

technical meaning being defined	=	generalised class with qualification
Acid rain	is	a chemical **phenomenon** (that is) caused by the dissolution of nitrogen oxides and sulphur dioxide in rainwater to form nitric acid and sulphuric acid.
Sea breezes	are	**movements** of air from the sea to the land (that are) caused by a difference in air temperature between the land and sea.
Air pollution	can be defined as	the **presence** of airborne particles that are harmful to the well-being of animal and plant life.
Nucleotides	can be understood as	the building **blocks** of nucleic acids.

generalised class with qualification	=	technical meaning being defined
This **movement** of air from the sea to the land	is called	a sea breeze.
Folds which bend upwards	are called	anticlines.
The **measure** of the radiation energy that is absorbed at the target site	is called	the radiation dose.
The **work** (that is) needed to accelerate a body of given mass from rest to its stated velocity	is defined as	the kinetic energy of an object.

Figure 35: Setting up technicalising relationships in definitions

Moving from a dynamic to a synoptic perspective on phenomena

The Laboratory Report was discussed as a macrogenre, moving from action in the method stage to reflection and generalisation in the discussion and conclusion stages. We could say that the Laboratory Report is essentially doing the same thing as the register continuum describes. Both step off from the dynamic world of actions with concrete things and with spoken language accompanying the actions. At the other end of the continuum, we have the world as a linguistic construct. At this end, language constitutes more static, or synoptic, meanings, where there is reflection on the world and relationships and theoretical concepts are constructed. Halliday (2003) has described this movement across the register continuum using the metaphor of weather and climate: weather is dynamic and continually changing, while climate is about generalised patterns of the weather in regions.

We could also think of the metaphor of a hot air balloon. When the balloon is on the ground, there are people darting around, fixing things, making sure the basket is filled correctly and making sure the gas is fired so the balloon is filled with hot air. In other words, the scene is one of action, with commands and concrete things, and there are people in charge and there are those who have to follow orders. Then, as the balloon rises, the possible meanings change. What were active individuals are now static pairs or groups observing the rising balloon and what were individual trees have become woods and then forests. A launching area is now a meadow and then a meadow becomes one of many fields where farming is carried out. As the balloon continues upwards, the farming patterns are recognisable, which are now talked about as agriculture and a house has become a village, which has become part of an urban region. The further the balloon goes up, the more generalised, abstract and technical the meanings are. The interest, now, is in relationships and definitions, perhaps geophysical or geographical, perhaps economic or mathematical. To get to this point, the dynamic language choices made when the balloon was on the ground are no longer viable. Those language resources cannot make the kinds of meanings we wish to make when the balloon is so high up. To construct abstract concepts and issues and, essentially, take a synoptic view of the world, we use a major resource in the language called nominalisation.

Nominalisation

Nominalisation is the process of changing the resources of a dynamic world, which is built around verbs, into the resources of a synoptic world, which is built around nouns.

Let us return to the teacher working with his students on digestion (Fig. 34). At some point in his students' learning, he wanted them to be able to express the following meaning: 'The emulsification of fats by bile results in their efficient digestion.' However, his likely starting point would have been something along the lines of:

> *'Bile breaks down fats by lowering their surface tension, which causes them to break up into tiny droplets. Note that the bile does not break down the fats chemically. Now that the fats are in the form of tiny droplets, their surface area has increased, which means that the enzyme, lipase, can now work on more fats at the same time and so digest them much more easily.'*

Register continuum

concrete, everyday, commonsense
informal, subjective, novice
language accompanying action, spoken

technical, abstract
formal, objective, expert
language as reflection, written

1. Bile breaks down fats by lowering their surface tension, which causes them to break up into tiny droplets. Note that the bile does not break down the fats chemically. Now that the fats are in the form of tiny droplets, their surface area has increased, which means that the enzyme, lipase, can now work on more fats at the same time and so digest them more easily .

The technical word we use instead of 'physically breaks down fats into tiny particles' is emulsify. So we can say that bile emulsifies fat.

Instead of 'easily', we should be more careful and say that it emulsifies the fats efficiently—that it does it quickly and with less energy.

2. Bile emulsifies fats by lowering their surface tension, which causes them to break up into tiny droplets. Now that the fats are in the form of tiny droplets, their surface area has increased, allowing the enzyme, lipase, to do its work faster and so digest the fats more efficiently.

Instead of 'Bile emulsifies fats', we can write 'The emulsification of fats by bile'.

Instead of 'digest the fats much more efficiently', we can write 'the efficient digestion of fat'.

Instead of 'so that', we can say 'results in' or 'resulting in'.

3a. The emulsification of fats by bile increases the rate at which lipase can work, resulting in the efficient digestion of fats.

3b. The emulsification of fats by bile results in their efficient digestion.

Figure 36: Scaffolding students into technicality and abstraction

Figure 36 shows a possible path taken by the teacher interacting with students in an attempt to move them from the left of the register continuum to the right. We see also that in changing something into a noun, we are forced to make other changes in the language.

The language of the first text in Figure 36 has the features typical of spoken language, which relies on the verbal group: many short clauses, short participants, processes of action and circumstances. In other words, it has grammatical intricacy and lexical simplicity (Halliday 1985). Texts 3a and 3b, in contrast, have features typical of written language: one clause or two clause sentences, expanded participants, fewer circumstances. In other words, grammatical simplicity and lexical complexity (high lexical density). This is observed in Text 3b, which is made up of a single clause with two participants on either side of a causal process, with a lexical density of six.

How does the shift occur in the grammar? We can see through the shaded texts that it occurs through several changes. One is the shift from less technical meanings to more technical ones such as 'breaks down' to 'emulsifies'. The other significant change is to nominalise processes: emulsify becomes emulsification, digest becomes digestion. Once we have emulsification, we can qualify it, 'emulsification of fats', and qualify again, 'emulsification of fats by bile'. Similarly, once we have digestion, we can qualify it, 'digestion of fats' and then describe it, 'efficient digestion of fats', and point to it, 'the efficient digestion of fats'.

Advantages of nominalisation

As we have seen, once verbs and adjectives have been changed into nouns, then what becomes available to the language user is the potential of the nominal group: to classify, describe, quantify, point to and qualify. For example, it is possible to:

- classify: ***radioactive*** *waste,* ***food*** *irradiation,* ***radiative heat*** *loss*
- quantify: *17% heat loss,* ***a 50%*** *increase*
- qualify: *The increased rate* ***of absorption in the small intestine*** *is due to…*

This is a powerful potential and it allows, for example, a process to become the do-er of an action. For example, once we change 'eats away' to 'corrodes' and then change that to 'corrosion', we can make 'corrosion' the cause of another event, such as 'Corrosion negatively affects the strength of materials and...'.

It is possible to change more than processes (realised through verbs) into entities (realised through nouns). For example, we can also change expressions of qualities ('efficient' becomes 'efficiency'), expressions of probability and frequency ('might' becomes 'probability' or 'risk', 'usually' becomes 'tendency' or 'frequency'), and expressions of logic ('because' becomes 'reason' or 'cause', 'so' becomes 'effect' or 'outcome').

Nominalisation of a process

Nominalisation can also be the sum of a number of actions that make up a process. Two examples are:

Sample 1

'The copper anodes are then taken to a refinery where they and stainless steel plates called cathodes are lowered into a special chemical bath that has electricity flowing through it. Copper transfers from the anode to the cathode and the end ***product*** *is pure copper sheets. This process is called* ***electro-refining****.'*

Sample 2

'Sometimes metal structures fail due to metal ***fatigue****, which is produced by the metal being subjected to repeated* ***loading and unloading*** *over a long period of time. Using and stressing the metal constantly may cause the metal to fail at some point. The time the metal takes to fail could be quickened by a flaw in the metal itself or if there is a design flaw or weak point in the structure. It is* ***this type of failure*** *that is called* ***metal fatigue****.'*

Notice in Sample 2 how nominalisations formed can be used at various points in the text and even on both sides of a definition: the technical term 'metal fatigue', which is introduced at the start, is defined in the end by saying it is a type of 'failure'.

Problems caused by nominalisation

Nominalisation can also cause problems. One of the problems is that sometimes it is difficult to identify, for example, who or what is doing something or what the cause is of a phenomenon.

In this following example, it is not clear how the food is transmitted. We can assume but we cannot be certain of our understanding. The version that comes after identifies more clearly what is going on.

> *'One way that pheromones are distributed between the worker bees and drones and the queen bee is through* ***food transmission behaviour****.'*

> *'One of the ways that the pheromones are shared with other worker bees and drones in the colony as well as fed back to the queen bee herself is by sharing food with each other…'*

However, that does not mean we should not use the term 'food transmission behaviour' because it allows us to say, for example: 'Food transmission behaviour varies from…'

The second problem is less an issue with nominalisation and more of an issue caused by the language user. Overuse can obfuscate meaning, so there is always a balancing act between wanting to package meanings in a certain way and making sure that clarity of expression is not lost.

Our reliance on nominalisations and the degree to how comfortable we feel with them in increasingly abstract and technical texts is clear when we see in Text 26 two paragraphs from the Consequential Explanation on air pollution (Text 11). The nominalisations are bolded.

Text 26

WHAT ARE THE CONSEQUENCES OF AIR POLLUTION IN HONG KONG?

Air **pollution** is increasingly a major **problem** for cities around the globe, including Shanghai, Beijing and Hong Kong. Air **pollution** can be defined as the **presence** of airborne particles that are harmful to the **well-being** of animal and plant **life**. The **quality** of **life** in Hong Kong is negatively affected by air **pollution** in several ways and they include: **degradation** of **visibility**, acid rain, and, more broadly, rising temperatures and **depletion** of the ozone layer.

Visibility degradation is caused by airborne particles, which scatter light and serve as **condensation** nuclei for clouds and fog. The particulates can come from natural **phenomena** such as volcanic **eruptions**, dust storms and sea spray or from human **activities** such as **combustion**. In Hong Kong, the **combustion** of fossil fuels in cars is the main **contributor** and the situation is worsened by the **occurrence** of photochemical smog, which is formed when smoke and exhaust fumes are trapped in a fog and undergo photochemical **reactions**.

Packing and unpacking nominalisations

In the science classroom, meanings are often moving from the spoken and more everyday to the specialised and then to the written and more technical and/or abstract, as in 'gets bigger' to 'expands' to 'expansion'. However, the argument was put forward that teachers need to be more explicit by, for example, denaturalising the naturalised. For many teachers, the naturalised is the nominalised form and can find it difficult at times to shift back from the nominalised so that they can scaffold students through more spoken interactions. We can see in the following examples (Fig. 37) what that would take. The bolded words in the first text are nominalisations while the bolded words in the second text make similar meanings without nominalised forms.

Packing through nominalisation	Unpacking the nominalisations
The **depletion** of the ozone layer reduces the **protection** from harmful UV light that the ozone layer provides humans. The ozone layer is between 12km and 50km above the earth's surface and is being depleted by chlorofluorocarbons (CFCs), which react to break down the ozone. Although **attempts** have been made to replace CFCs, they are still used as aerosol propellants, solvents, and refrigerants. **Reducing the concentration** of ozone will lead to greater amounts of UVB reaching the earth. This may cause problems such as skin cancers, eye disease and gene **mutation**.	If the ozone layer **becomes thinner and thinner**, then it won't be able **to protect** us from harmful UV light. The ozone layer is between 12km and 50km above the earth's surface and the number of ozone molecules is being reduced by chlorofluorocarbons (CFCs), which react to break down the ozone. Although people **have tried** to replace CFCs, they are still used in aerosol containers, as solvents, and to refrigerate. If we **thin** the ozone layer further, then greater amounts of UVB will reach the earth. More UVB may cause skin cancers, eye disease and may even cause genes **to mutate**.

Figure 37: Similar meanings expressed with or without nominalisations

How teachers scaffold students to move between the two was taken up in the discussions around meso-scaffolding and micro-scaffolding.

Using lexical cohesion to develop understanding of the field

The technical terms that construct a field, especially in the describing and organising genres, may seem overwhelming to students who are in the early stages of learning the field. The first reaction to new vocabulary may be to write up lists of the new words encountered — they usually include the new words that have been bolded by the writers of a text book. However, simply listing words does not take advantage of the fact that the knowledge is patterned. Using the existing patterns of knowledge in a text would arguably be a more efficient way of learning and recalling technical terms; more like a thesaurus approach than an individual word in a dictionary, although dictionaries are important. We will explore a way of using the relationships between content words, termed lexical relations. A benefit of this for students is that having the teacher go through the process actively with the class provides the students with opportunities to recycle the language of the text, including words they know the meaning of but also incorporating the new terms.

Developing vocabulary by working with lexical relations

A text hangs together, or is made cohesive, through the use of a number of resources in the language, such as pronouns (e.g. it, these) and cohesive conjunctions (e.g. However, Therefore, ...). Another major way is through the various relations that can be set up between lexical items. These relations could be one of being alike or of not being alike, or of belonging to a class of things, and of being a component of something bigger. We can now explore all of these lexical relations (Fig. 38) using the text, 'Animals of the Sea', which is an example of a Classification.

ANIMALS OF THE SEA

Marine animals are divided into three groups: zooplankton, nekton, and benthos. Zooplankton are drifting animals, which are unable to propel themselves effectively and are, therefore, at the mercy of either wind or current. They are usually small but can grow to a fairly large size; the jellyfish and the Portuguese man-of-war are examples of larger types of zooplankton. The zooplankton population also includes some temporary members such as fish eggs or larval forms of organisms, which may grow up and leave the planktonic community to join the nekton or benthos.

Nekton are free swimmers, and the largest portion of familiar animals found in the ocean probably belong to this class. Common fishes, the octopus, whales, eels and squid are all examples of nekton. The nekton category includes a number of very diverse creatures. The whale, dolphin and porpoise are certainly very different from codfish or trout because whales represent sea mammals, whereas cod are true fishes.

The third type of sea animal spends its entire life on or in the ocean bottom. This group of marine animals is called the benthos. It includes lobsters, starfish, various worms, snails, oysters and many more. Some of these creatures, such as lobsters and snails, may be able to move about on the bottom but their lifestyle is so bound up with the ocean floor that they are unable to survive away from this environment.

Lexical relations

Words that are related to water:
marine, ocean, sea

Words that set up classes of animals of the sea and members of that class:

zooplankton
drifting animals, jellyfish, Portuguese man-of-war, fish eggs, larval forms of organisms, planktonic

nekton
free swimmers, (familiar animals), common fishes, octopus, whales, eels, squid, dolphin, porpoise, codfish, trout, sea mammals, true fishes

benthos
lobsters, starfish, worms, snails, oysters

Words that express movement:
drifting, propel, free swimmers, move about, float, swim, (*live*).

Words that are related to groups:
groups, types, population, members, community, portion, class, examples, category.

Adapted from http://legacy.mos.org/oceans/life/surface.html (Accessed 30 January 2016)

Figure 38: Using lexical relations as a strategy for developing vocabulary

If all of the words in the column on the right of the text were highlighted within the text, we would see that almost all the content words in the text would be highlighted. This tells us that this text is essentially made up of four sets of lexical items or lexical chains. Within each of those chains might be smaller groupings.

Expressing cause and effect

Causal relations are arguably the driving logical relation in science. As such, developing control of the resources in the language for explicitly expressing the causal links is crucial. The focus, here, is on explicit expressions (bolded), although it must be stated that there is implicitly expressed cause, too.

Text 27

The light bulb glows dimly or stops glowing **because** the current flowing through it is too small. Now, nearly all of the current flows through wire S **since** it has a much lower resistance than the light bulb.

Text 27 has cause expressed explicitly twice (because, since) and it is a simple task to identify what the causes and the effects are on either side of the causal relation. However, there is a causal relation (because) in this text that is not expressed explicitly. The implicit causal relation is the link that exists between 'the current flowing through it is too small' and 'Now, nearly all of the current flows through wire S'. As we can see, we have the cause and we have the effect but an explicit language element, such as 'because', that would identify the causal relation is not there. This implicit causality can be difficult for a reader who is new to the field.

What are some of the resources available for expressing causal relations? We can identify a range of resources simply by analysing some text extracts. The explicit causal resources in the following texts are in bold, while any resource that is not explicitly causal is in italics.

Text 28

Since the water outside has a higher water potential than the pear cells, water moves into the cells. The incoming water *increases* the water content of the cells. **As a result**, more fruit juice can be extracted.

Text 28 has two examples of explicit cause. One is a conjunction that joins two clauses (since) and the other is a conjunction that joins larger chunks of meanings, that is, two sentences (As a result). There is also an implicit causal meaning and it is expressed by 'increases'. To understand its causal meaning, one has to understand that there is a cause, 'water moving into cells', and an effect, 'the water content of the cells'. If we reworded it, we could express the cause explicitly as: 'water moves into the cells, **resulting in** an increase in the water content of the cells'.

Text 29

When the metal rod is heated, the particles at the hot end vibrate faster. The fast vibrating particles bump into the slower, neighbouring particles and **make** them vibrate more rapidly. *As* this bumping process continues, all the particles in the metal rod vibrate faster.

The explicit causal resource in Text 29 is perhaps not so easily recognisable as a causal process but if we replaced it with 'causes', we could have more obviously '**causes** them to vibrate'. The less obvious ones in italics express both time and cause. If we removed the temporal meaning and isolated the causal, we could have clearer causal expressions, '**Because** the metal rod is heated' and '**Because** this bumping continues'

With the next sample text, Text 30, the majority of the causal resources are explicit and are realised through nominals (result, effect) and processes (lead to, resulting in). In this text, an implicit causal meaning is expressed through 'allows'. Again, it can be replaced with a more obvious example such as 'leads to' so we have 'which **results in** certain radiation entering the glasshouse …'

Text 30

Rising temperatures are the major **result** of the greenhouse **effect**, which, in turn, **lead to** droughts and increasing sea levels. The greenhouse **effect** is the name given to the atmosphere behaving in the same way as a greenhouse, which *allows* certain radiation to enter the glasshouse but stops other radiation escaping. More precisely, objects on the earth absorb UV light and emit low-energy infra-red radiation, which is trapped by the earth's atmosphere, **resulting in** increased temperatures. The **effect** is worsened when the atmosphere is concentrated with air particles and/or pollutants such as water vapour, carbon monoxide, carbon dioxide and methane.

Resources for expressing causal relations

Language resources	Examples
Causal conjunctions	• Conjunctions that join clauses to make sentences: *because, so, since, as, so, …* • Conjunctions that join sentences and paragraphs: *Therefore, Thus, As a result, As a consequence, …*
Causal processes	*results in, leads to, causes, produces, …*
Causal prepositions	*because of, due to, …*
Causal nominals	*cause, reason, factor, effect, consequence, outcome, product, …*

Figure 39: Language resources for expressing cause

Writing a Sequential Explanation

To see how this understanding of causality can be taken up in the science classroom, we will take an example designed in collaboration with a science teacher who wanted to model and deconstruct for his students how to write a Sequential Explanation that not only flowed well but also expressed explicit and comprehensive causality.

The context is a circuit in which a light bulb is connected and glows. When a wire (wire S) is attached to the circuit on either side of the globe, the globe either glows dimly or stops glowing altogether and the student is required to explain this phenomenon. Figure 40 shows the model response provided in the classroom and the process taken to get to that final text.

The teacher began with a clause at a time and asked why that event happened, answered that question with a statement that began with 'because' and continued in that manner.

Teacher's modelling of the phases in the Sequential Explanation through questions		**Explain why the light bulb glows dimly or stops glowing**
What do you see? ······▶		The light bulb glows dimly or stops glowing
Why does the light bulb glow dimly or stop glowing? ······▶	because	the current that is flowing through it is too small
Why is the current too small? ······▶	because	now nearly all of the current flows through wire S
Why does nearly all the current flow through wire S? ······▶	because	it has a much lower resistance than the wire in the light bulb.

First 'draft'

The light bulb glows dimly or stops glowing because the current flowing through it is too small because nearly all of the current flows through wire S because it has a much lower resistance than the light bulb.

Figure 40: Sample modelling and deconstruction of a short Sequential Explanation

Once everything was laid out, the teacher took the students through a process (Fig. 41) of 'editing' the text so that it ended up being the desired model Sequential Explanation.

Teacher's suggestions for editing the text

Teacher's suggestions	Text
Omit 'that is' and 'the wire in' in the fourth line.	**First 'draft'** The light bulb glows dimly or stops glowing because the current flowing through it is too small because nearly all of the current flows through wire S because it has a much lower resistance than the light bulb.
Construct two sentences from the four clauses (two clauses per sentence).	**Second 'draft'** The light bulb glows dimly or stops glowing because the current flowing through it is too small. Now, nearly all of the current flows through wire S because it has a much lower resistance than the light bulb.
Choose 'since' as an alternative to 'because'.	**Final version** The light bulb glows dimly or stops glowing because the current flowing through it is too small. Now, nearly all of the current flows through wire S since it has a much lower resistance than the light bulb.

Figure 41: A teacher's modelled editing of a co-constructed Sequential Explanation

Note that this Sequential Explanation begins with the observation of the phenomenon. In other words, the students observe that the bulb glows dimly or doesn't glow so the question is why and then that is responded to, which elicits another why and so on. The flow is effect followed by cause. This is in contrast to many Sequential Explanations, which move in the opposite way, from cause to effect, and in which the implication sequence is one of 'so'. For example, we could rewrite the above text so that it flows according to cause then effect:

'Wire S has a much lower resistance than the wire in the light bulb, **so** nearly all the current flows through wire S instead, **so** the amount of current flowing through the filament in the bulb is too small, **so** it does not glow or it glows dimly.'

The wording of the task, 'Explain why the light bulb glows dimly or stops glowing in the circuit when we add wire S', does not demand the text to flow either way. This seems to be possible in physics, for example, where transformations may not be of interest or even possible. However, in biology or chemistry, where materials undergo some kind of change to form a new product, we often have to go from the 'beginning' to the 'end'. For example, when considering digestion, the teacher does not ask the students to look at the faecal material and explain how that came to be. The process starts with the food being ingested and then continues phase by phase through the process of digestion to the end of the process. Life cycles also go in one direction.

There were two observations about this modelling and deconstruction that were made and the first was that the desire to have 2 clauses only per sentence meant that the previously explicit causal meaning between the second clause and the third clause became implicit. That is, *'the current flowing through it is too small because now nearly all of the current flows through wire S'* has become *'the current flowing through it is too small. Now, nearly all of the current flows through wire S'* and the reader has to work harder to understand that there is a 'because' between 'small' and 'Now'.

The other observation was that the process scaffolded the students so well that subsequent independent constructions of Sequential Explanations were much improved. The sample student text that comes later in the book (Text 35) is indicative of what students are able to do with the appropriate scaffolding.

Language resources that determine the flow of texts

We have looked at generic structures and how they organise knowledge at the whole-text level. But clause-level resources for structuring meanings and ensuring they flow well also exist. The language resources for doing this are theme and rheme and the metaphor used to talk about what they are functioning to do is orientation.

The orientation of the messages help move the text forward and using the term, orientation, helps us visualise the organisation of the information in a message so we are prepared by the speaker or writer for what is about to come. The macro-patterns of what speakers and writers choose will depend on the genre, as well as what has come before and what is coming next. This helps build a coherent text and, most times, the choices allow for smooth waves and a calm flow from one message to the next but, at times, choices are consciously made to disrupt the usual flow in order to signal a change.

In science, the genre that demands tight control of the orientations so that the texts flow well is the Sequential Explanation. As we will see, if the orientations are not chosen judiciously, understanding by the reader and listener is made much more difficult. This is significant for both teachers and students in terms of how they work with Sequential Explanations in the classroom so that learning of the phenomena being explained is successful.

Choices of orientation at the clause level

In English, the orientation to the message is achieved through what is placed at the front of the clause. This is called the theme of the clause and it includes everything from the start of the clause and up to but not including the process (Martin & Rose 2007), as indicated in the four examples below with the boundary identified with the upright slash | . Rheme is the remaining part of the clause and its function is generally to develop the orientation by giving new information. The exception to having the theme only up to but not including the process is the imperative mood clause, where the process is included as theme. We have various choices for theme and each choice makes a different meaning (Fig. 42), however slight.

Theme: the orientation to the message

(a)	The authorities | released the drug after an exhaustive clinical trial.
(b)	The drug | was released by the authorities after an exhaustive clinical trial.
(c)	After an exhaustive clinical trial, the authorities | released the drug.
(d)	After an exhaustive clinical trial, the drug | was released by the authorities.

Figure 42: Varying the orientations in a clause

Each of the four clauses in Figure 42 has a different orientation, although the difference between (c) and (d) is that they each have a different minor orientation.

What motivates each of those choices to be made? Example (a) would probably be chosen if the meaning was intended to say something about the authorities. It could be a response to 'So, were the authorities careful about releasing the drug?' and by having an orientation to the authorities, this is achieved. Example (b) would be the typical choice if the text unfolded according to the drug; for example, in response to 'So the drug was released when?' Lastly, with their major orientation to time, examples (c) and (d) would be motivated by having to recount a major event or series of events. Then, once the time has been established, a minor orientation has been chosen, either the authorities or the drug, and the motivations for those are similar to the ones already given for (a) and (b).

We can see that, despite almost the exact same words being used in all four examples, the meanings are not the same. In terms of experiential meanings (linked to field), they are the same and, with respect to interpersonal meanings (linked to tenor), they are the same because they are all statements and there is no added uncertainty, for example. So what is different is in the textual meanings (linked to mode) — the arrangement of the clauses so that the orientations make new meanings.

Orientation to technicality and abstraction

The notion of orientation was referred to when macro-scaffolding was discussed and two options each for Procedural Recounts and for Explanations with human agency were given. The difference between each option was whether the orientation was to the scientist or the science. In the examples given above (Fig. 42), it could be said that (a) and (b) vary according to whether the orientation is to the authorities or the drug. However, what happens if the writer wants the orientation to be to some kind of technicality or abstraction that might have been expressed in a more spoken form through verbs and adjectives? Figure 43 compares two different constructions. The first construes a more dynamic world of layers of changing thicknesses, and of chemicals and whether they are going to protect us or allow the UV light to hurt us. The second is a more static world where some of the goings on in the world are now construed in more abstract ways such as depletion and protection.

(a)	If **the ozone layer** | becomes thinner and thinner, // **then it** | won't be able to protect us from harmful UV light.
(b)	**The depletion of the ozone layer** | reduces the protection from harmful UV light that the ozone layer provides humans.

Figure 43: Nominalisation allows us further options in the orientation of messages.

We see that it is by nominalising 'the ozone layer becomes thinner and thinner' as 'the depletion of the ozone layer' that the writer has been able to package the cause of the problem in a nominal group. And that allows the language user to put the cause neatly at the front as the orientation for what they wish to say, that is, that the depletion reduces the protection.

Keep in mind that one cannot choose an action as an orientation in the verb form unless it is in the imperative mood, typically expressing a command. For example, if one wanted the orientation to be to the act of eroding, then 'erode' cannot be chosen because it would indeed be a meaning that would belong more appropriately in drama or poetry: 'Erode the banks, ye mighty river!' But, if erode is nominalised to erosion, then it is possible to have the action of erosion as the orientation, such as:

Erosion | is a major problem in agriculture.
Erosion | reduces available soil moisture.

In the first example, erosion as the orientation means that

it can then be commented on, it's a problem. In the second example, erosion can be seen as the actor of the action or the cause itself, 'erosion does this to soil moisture'.

Orientation to causal meanings

Nominalisation brings with it the potential to not only choose a variety of orientations but also to expand the nominal groups that the nominalisations have formed and to choose to have the text flow according to causes or effects, as we saw with the orientation of depletion in Figure 43. Let us take the following sentence, which is made up of three clauses (identified with double forward slashes //).

People | are using optical fibres more and more //
because they | are more efficient than copper wiring, //
which | is thick, bulky and expensive. //

The orientations of these three clauses are people, optical fibres (they) and copper wiring (which), respectively. Instead of orientations to tangible things, we can nominalise some of the terms as in the following:

		nominalisation
are using *(a verb)*	*becomes*	the use
efficient *(an adjective)*	*becomes*	the efficiency
because *(a conjunction)*	*becomes*	the reason

Once the nominalisations have been formed, they can act as a packaged cause and effect and then chosen to be the orientation (Fig. 44).

Orientating the effect

(a)	The use of optical fibres | has increased // because they | are more efficient than thick, bulky and expensive copper wiring.
(b)	The increased use of optical fibres | is due to their greater efficiency over thick, bulky and expensive copper wiring.
(c)	The increase in the use of optical fibres | is due to their greater efficiency over thick, bulky and expensive copper wiring.
(d)	The reason for the increased use of optical fibres | is their greater efficiency over thick, bulky and expensive copper wiring.

Orientating the cause

(e)	Because of their efficiency over thick, bulky and expensive copper wiring, the use of optical fibres | has increased.
(f)	The inefficiency of thick, bulky and expensive copper wiring | has led to an increased use of optical fibre.

Figure 44: Changing the orientations to cause or effect

It is clear in the first examples, where the orientation is to the effect, how the nominal group formed with the abstraction 'use' is able to be expanded and worked with in multiple ways. In (a), it is qualified with 'of optical fibres', and then in (b) what was previously a verb is now used as a describer, 'increased'. Then in (c) the verb 'to increase' is nominalised to 'the increase' and 'the use' has now been shifted to act as part of the qualifier 'in the use of optical fibres'. The conjunction 'because' is nominalised to 'reason' and now that is made the thing of the new nominal group. In summary, (a) and (b) have 'use' as the orientations, (c) has 'increase', and (d) has 'reason' as the orientation. All of them are abstractions and all of them allow for technicality to be included through the qualifier, and all of them allow the writer the option of orientating the message to the effect.

With the cause as orientation in (e) and (f), the themes are built around the abstract cause, 'inefficiency', seeing as that is the reason for optical fibre's increased use, as stated here.

Ensuring Sequential Explanations flow well

Sequential Explanations are crucial in science. School curricula, textbooks, assignments and exams continually demand that students explain why and how certain scientific phenomena occur. For many topics covered in school science, it is not enough that students know the characteristics of a phenomenon; they need to consider questions such as: 'How does that happen?' or 'Why does that happen?' Sequential Explanations in science function to explain the sequence of events that constitute a physical phenomenon and the fact that it is a sequence of events places pressure on the language to be organised so that the meanings flow clearly and as efficiently as possible. If the language is organised well, through judicious use of the theme, then the work for the teacher and students is made much easier. But what content constitutes the theme in Sequential Explanations? For this, we go to another system in the language and that is the one that tells us that the information that is chosen to be theme is usually the information that is familiar or that has been given previously in the text. Text 31, which is a student text, illustrates how this flow is achieved in the explanation sequence stage of the text. The first sentence identifies the phenomenon so the explanation sequence starts from the second sentence.

Text 31

THE EFFECT OF DENSITY CHANGE

A submarine with the same density as sea water is moving in the sea.

When the pump is turned on, it draws water away from the submarine.

As the water is pumped away, the amount of water inside the submarine decreases.

As the amount of water inside the submarine decreases, the density of the submarine decreases so that it is lower than the sea water outside.

Since the submarine now has lower density than the sea water, it floats to the top of the sea.

It is clear in Text 31 that the result of an action becomes the beginning of the next action. In other words, elements in the previous rheme are repackaged as the theme of the next clause. To underline the need to carefully choose the content of the theme, let us consider an example of a classroom text (Text 32) whose choices of theme were inappropriate for a Sequential Explanation because they did not set up a sequence of events. Instead, they set up static pieces of information, which would be appropriate for an example of a Component but not for a Sequential Explanation.

Text 32

HOW DOES THE HUMAN EAR WORK?

The pinna | collects the sound waves.

Then the ear canal | directs the sound waves to the eardrum.

They | hit the eardrum

and (they) | make it vibrate.

The ear bones | amplify the vibrations from the eardrum

and (they) | pass them on to the inner ear.

The cochlea | changes the vibrations into electrical messages in the inner ear.

The auditory nerves | carry these messages to the brain.

The brain | interprets these messages as sounds.

The class activity which used this text had the text cut into strips with each sentence on a separate strip. The students were required to organise the jumbled strips to construct the original text. Despite this rather straightforward exercise, half the class had trouble putting it together. Later, when the text was analysed, it was found that the pattern of orientations does not explain how the ear works; rather, the orientations are to the various components of the ear — appropriate for the Component genre but not for a Sequential Explanation. However, if the orientations are changed so that there is a flow, the result is something like Text 33, instead.

Text 33

The pinna | collects the sound waves.

These sound waves | are directed by the ear canal to the eardrum.

The eardrum | is hit by the sound waves,

which | make it vibrate.

The vibrations | are amplified by the ear bones in the middle ear

and they | pass on to the cochlea.

The cochlea | changes the vibrations into electrical messages.

These electrical messages | are carried by the auditory nerve to the brain

which | interprets the messages as sounds.

This text does explain the chain of events making up a phenomenon by having the necessary flow and this has been achieved by having the new information (in the rhemes) being taken up as given information in the subsequent theme. We could reword it by using 'which' and show how most of the rhemes and adjacent themes are one and the same.

The pinna | collects the sound waves,

which | are directed by the ear canal to the eardrum,

which | is hit by the sound waves,

which | make it vibrate.

The vibrations | are amplified by the ear bones

and they | pass on to the cochlea,

which | changes the vibrations into electrical messages,

which | are carried by the auditory nerve to the brain,

which | interprets the messages as sounds.

Representing this flow more diagrammatically so that we can insert arrows, we have Figure 45, which makes clear how the flow is achieved. This kind of diagram is a good illustration of why both science teachers and students should have an understanding of the language patterns in their discipline and the visual presentation of those language patterns.

HOW DOES THE HUMAN EAR WORK?

The pinna | collects the sound waves.

These sound waves | are directed by the ear canal to the eardrum.

The eardrum | is hit by the sound waves

which | make it vibrate.

The vibrations | are amplified by the ear bones in the middle ear

and they | pass on to the cochlea.

The cochlea | changes the vibrations into electrical messages.

These electrical messages | are carried by the auditory nerve to the brain,

which | interprets the messages as sounds.

Figure 45: The patterns of flow in explaining how the human ear works

As mentioned previously, there is considerable linguistic pressure when writing an explanation of dynamic processes in the physical world. One way of mitigating that pressure is to ensure a close relationship between the visual and verbal texts. In other words, breaking up the verbal text into the phases of the phenomenon and situating them within the visual text. In another science classroom, the students had the cross-section first (Fig. 46), learned the functions of each of the component parts of the ear and then, as they worked through the Explanation, they wrote each phase in the text boxes. The blue line shows how the flow of the text helps in its reading.

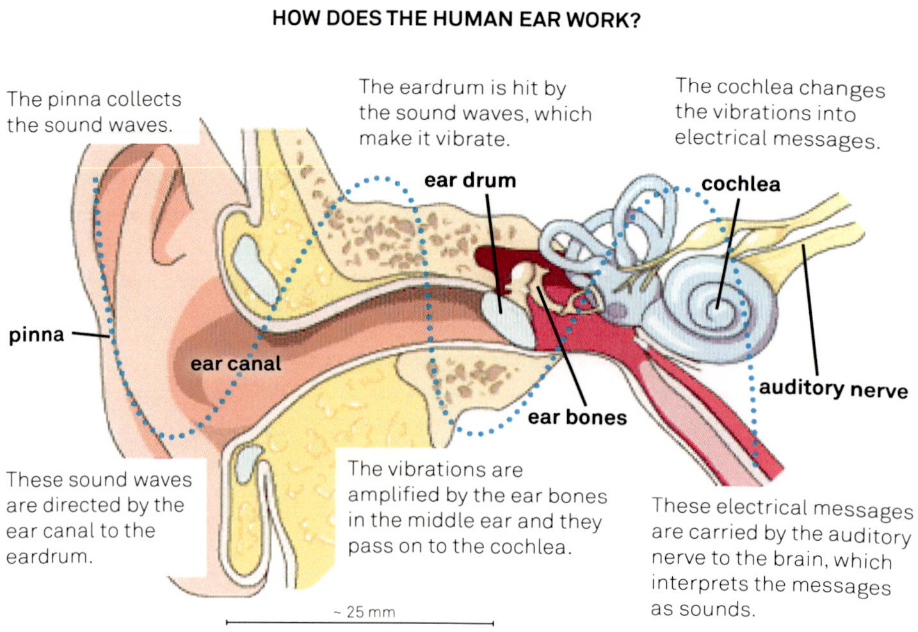

Figure 46: A visual scaffold for teaching a Sequential Explanation

Three more examples that illustrate the value of having the phases in the verbal text closely aligned with the visual text are Texts 34, 35 and 36.

Text 34 was a teacher's second attempt at modelling and deconstructing a Sequential Explanation, making visually explicit to the students how the new information in each phase becomes the given in the next phase.

Text 34

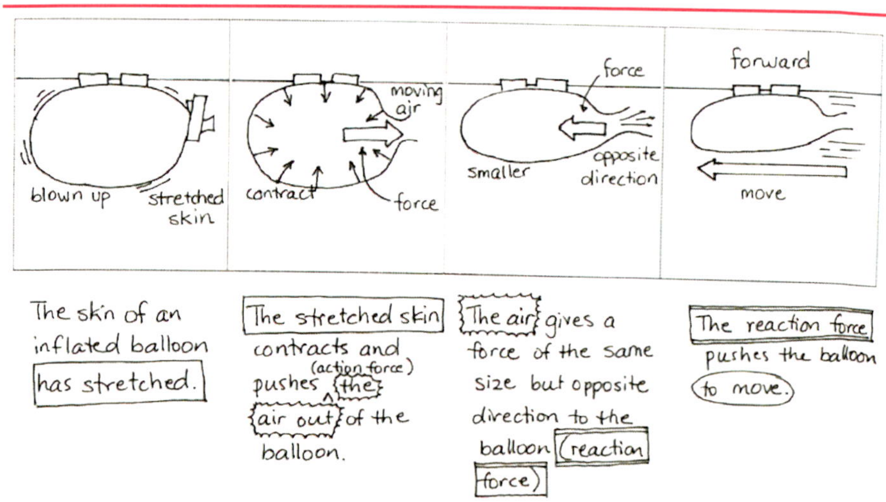

A product of the work in the classroom of the teacher who started with Text 34 is the student text on the effect of density change (Text 35). The report on the teacher's and students' work (Polias 2007b) shows that the teaching of the flow of Sequential Explanations is not something that is learned in a lesson or two but takes time.

Text 35

THE EFFECT OF DENSITY CHANGE

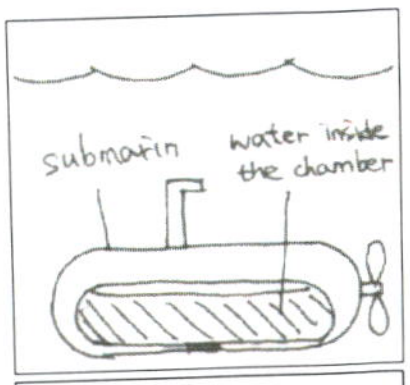

A submarine with the same density as sea water is moving in the sea.

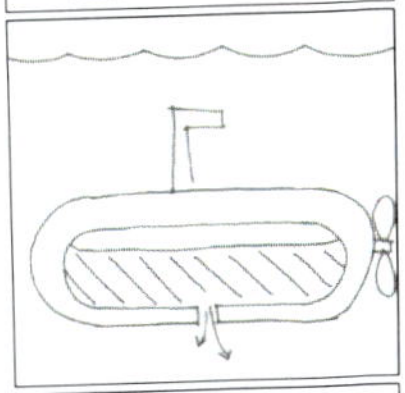

When the pump is turned on, it draws water away from the submarine.

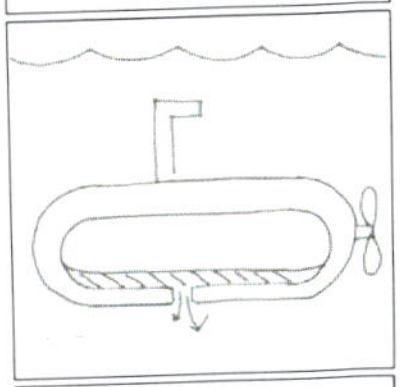

As the water is pumped away, the amount of water inside the submarine decreases.

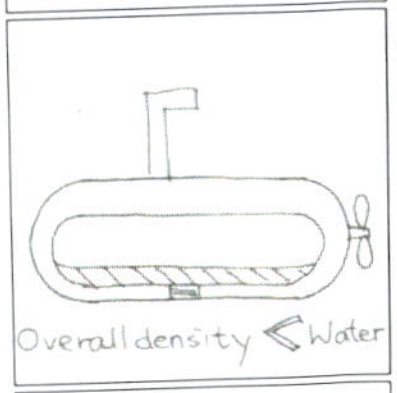

As the amount of water inside the submarine decreases, the density of the submarine decreases so that it is lower than the sea water outside.

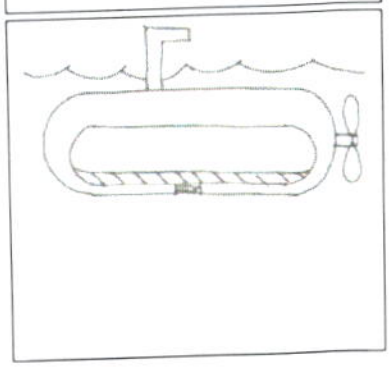

Since the submarine now has lower density than the sea water, it floats to the top of the sea.

The teacher and students had worked on several Sequential Explanations (on air cushions reducing friction, action and reaction force, and fuses) and the text here is a product after several lessons and over a month or so. The first two phases in the Explanation were written by the teacher, while the students needed to write the last three phases.

This next example (Text 36) is adapted from a text written by a student on the topic of how geothermal energy is produced. With each phase of the verbal text numbered and located in the visual text, and with colour used so the phenomenon and deduction stages (purple shade) are distinguished from the explanation sequence, we can see how much it benefits the reader. Also, when the text is read as it follows the diagram, it is easy to identify which part of the geothermal energy process is not addressed in the verbal text but is in the visual text. What we see is that the verbal text is not concerned with the recycling of the water, from the turbines to the condensers, cooling towers and re-injection wells.

Text 36

GEOTHERMAL ENERGY

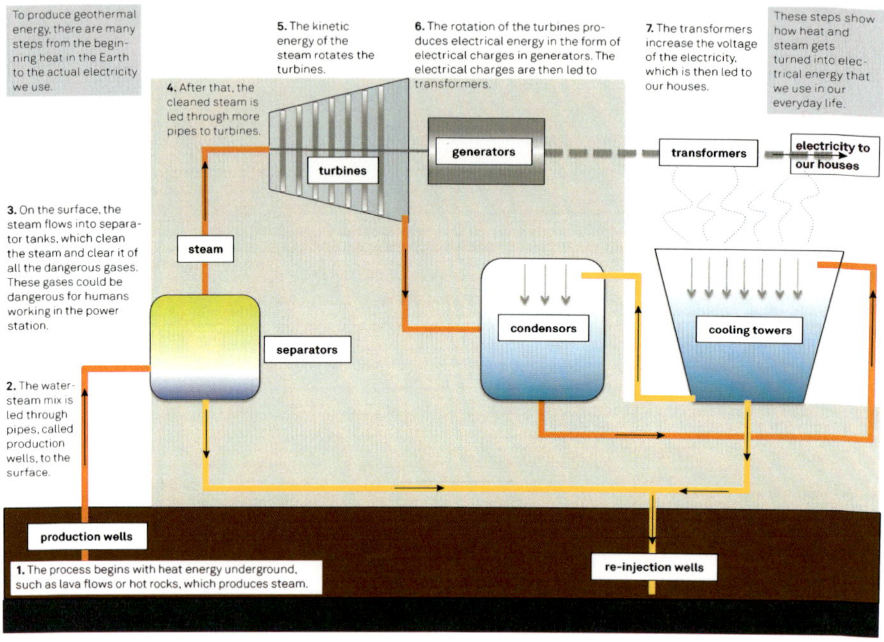

Written text adapted from a student text: Bjarne Bombach, Nov 2012. Used with permission.

Repackaging the new as the given

Many Sequential Explanations in school science, especially in biology, are comprised of many processes where there are clearly new products formed, either through the combination of materials or through growth or development of some kind. We will look at two of these: the frog life-cycle and digestion.

Text 37

THE FROG LIFE CYCLE

When frogs mate, the female lays eggs in water and the male sheds sperm over the eggs to fertilize them. The fertilized eggs look like balls of jelly with a black dot in the middle of each of them.

About one to three weeks later, the eggs hatch into tadpoles, which breathe using their gills and move like a fish with their long tails.

By the time they are about 6 weeks old, the external gills have disappeared and the tadpoles begin to develop lungs.

Around two weeks later, the tadpoles form hind legs, their bodies become longer and their heads become more distinct and more frog-like.

After about 12 weeks, the almost mature froglets start to grow front legs and lose their tails. Their lungs are fully developed for breathing.

Eventually, the mature frog has lost its tail completely and, as an adult, is able to live on land.

Clearly, Text 37 unfolds according to time with elements of time coming at the front of all the phases in the explanation sequence, e.g. 'when frogs mate', 'about one to three weeks later', 'by the time they are about 6 weeks old'. However, although having a text unfolding according to time is appropriate and sufficient for Recounts, that pattern is not sufficient for a Sequential Explanation. And so, once the time has been established, it is the development of the frog through its various phases that is focused on. In the first phase, the egg-laying phase, it has the adult frogs as the given and presents the eggs as the new. The next phase, the egg-hatching phase, takes the previous phase's new, the eggs, as its given and produces the tadpoles as the new. Throughout Text 55 is the same pattern of picking up the new information in the previous phase and making that the given information in the next phase. That is how the cycle continues. In fact, that is how a cycle must continue if it is to express the development or transformation that happens in a cycle, whether that is a life cycle or something such as the rain cycle.

In attempting to explain digestion, a text co-constructed by a class (Text 38) ended up with 'food' as the orientation in the first four clauses. It is only in the last two clauses that there is a change in orientation to the new product (protein, fats and starch) from the previous phases. This is similar to the problem with Text 32, in which the flow does not move according to the transformations of the food in the digestive processes. This puts the teaching and learning at risk. Text 39 is then a reworked version — the transformations are explicit, the flow is achieved and so the process of digestion is clearer to the reader.

Text 38

First version

DIGESTION OF FOOD IN HUMANS

Food | is broken down into smaller particles by teeth. Food | is broken down by enzymes present in the saliva. Food | is pushed down in the stomach by the contraction of muscles. Food | is mixed with digestive juices // to break down the proteins into smaller particles. Protein, fats and starch | are broken down into smaller pieces // so that they | can be used by the body.

Text 39

Revised version

DIGESTION OF FOOD IN HUMANS

The digestion process | begins in the mouth, // where the food | is chewed into smaller particles by the teeth. These particles of food | are further broken down by enzymes present in the saliva // to form balls of food called boluses. The boluses | are squeezed down towards the stomach by the contraction of muscles in the oesophagus. In the stomach, the boluses | mix with digestive juices, // resulting in the proteins in the boluses breaking down into small particles. These partially digested food particles | move into the first part of the small intestine...

Note that the revised version is more technical than the first version. That is another benefit of ensuring the text flows so well that the dynamic process is easy for the student to follow; the technicality can be increased and yet the meanings are still accessible to the student. As was stated previously, simulations and visuals, and placing each phase of the text next to the relevant visual is crucial for students. It has not been done here but one could envisage a cross-section of the human body with the components of the digestive system identified and labelled and each phase of the digestive process located in its relevant place.

As we complete this section on Sequential Explanations, we conclude that, if students are to be able to write well-constructed examples, then two linguistic resources are required: being able to nominalise and to use the passive voice. These two resources open up choices that would otherwise make it difficult if not impossible.

If we consider nominalisation first, we can see that to be able to write Text 33, it is necessary for vibrates to be nominalised to vibrations for that action to be the orientation to the next meaning. If we do not nominalise vibrates, then the writer is forced to revert to 'the ear bones', but we have already seen (Text 32) that that is the choice more typical of a Component than a Sequential Explanation. The same happens in phase 6 of Text 36, where the steam rotating the turbines is nominalised to 'The rotation of the turbines'.

When we consider active or passive voice, it is what constitutes theme that determines which voice is to be used. If in Text 39, the writer wants the orientation of the first phase to be the food, then the passive 'is chewed' is needed. Otherwise, to use the active voice, it would be something like, 'We chew the food ...'. In Text 33, four of the nine clauses demand the passive voice to be used. For students who do not have control of the passive voice at the point where they are studying these phenomena in English, then this is significant in determining when the passive voice is taught explicitly.

Teaching the passive voice

The discussion above has been about when to use the passive voice and why it is needed. The following outlines a method of teaching students how to construct the passive voice (Custance, Dare & Polias 2011). First, the processes and participants are identified by asking questions and using colour and then the two participants in the clause are identified as either the do-er of the action or the receiver of the action, the done-to (Fig. 47). When the do-er is the orientation, it is called the active voice and no extra elements in the grammar are necessary. However, when the done-to is the orientation, then it is called the passive voice and certain grammatical elements are necessary.

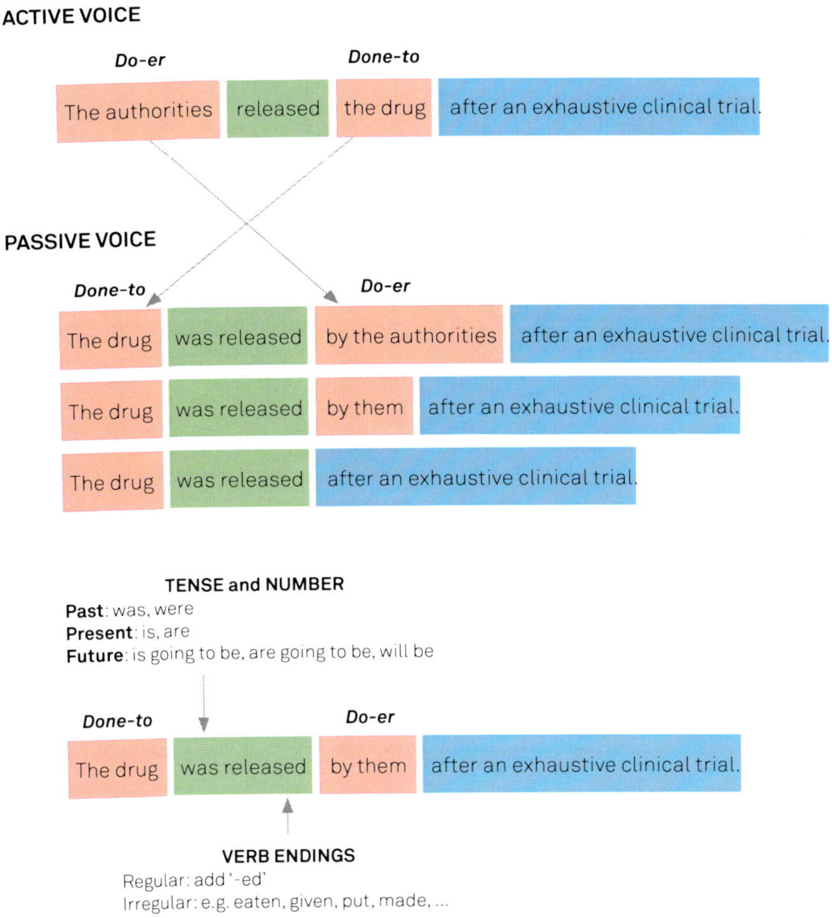

Figure 47: Arrangement of participants in the active and passive voices

Figure 47 shows that the first element in the verbal group in the passive voice has an element that expresses tense and number; this is almost always a form of the verb 'to be'. So, if we change the tense and keep it singular, we could have: '**was** released', '**is** released' and '**is going to be** released'. If we now make it plural, we could have '**were** released', '**are** released' and '**are going to be** released'.

As we can see, the lexical (or content) part of the verbal group, 'released', has the same form no matter what tense is chosen. The form the lexical part takes is the same as the lexical part used in, for example, 'have released', 'have chewed', 'have begun', 'have done'. If we use this last example in the passive voice, we could get, 'It **was done** according to the instructions.'

The 'by' is the new element that we attach to the do-er and, as Figure 46 shows, the do-er can be omitted when it is not the orientation, 'The drug was released (by the authorities) after an exhaustive clinical trial.'

Orientations in genres other than Sequential Explanations

Orientations in Descriptions

The orientations of the clauses in the organising and describing genres were presented before as typically being the topic or aspects of the topic being described or classified. That means that the orientations of the text on the sea eagle would typically be the sea eagle or aspects of the sea eagle's life. That is one of the reasons that the note-taking framework for Descriptions would have included bullet points; we know that the bullet point stands for the topic of the text and so do not have to keep on repeating it.

However, is there a bigger level of orientation than the one at the clause level? As Martin (1992: 437) suggests, we could look at a set of relationships such as: theme is to clause, as hyper-theme is to paragraph, as macro-theme is to whole text. In other words, there are 3 levels of orientation: for clause, paragraph, and whole text. The hyper-theme is known traditionally as topic sentence and the macro-theme as the introduction, but it seems more helpful to see each as an orientation at their respective levels. In other words, by using the concepts of macro-theme and hyper-theme, the writer (and reader) understands that the beginning part of the text is orientating the reader to what is coming in the whole text and the beginning part of a paragraph is orientating the reader to what is coming in the paragraph. And then, at the clause and clause complex level, the theme is orientating the reader to the message in that clause and clause complex. The terms introduction and topic sentence don't seem to set up the relationship as neatly.

For Descriptions, the hyper-themes are often realised by sub-headings and, typically, the beginning sentence or sentences. The shaded parts in Figure 48 show that the sub-headings of the Sea Eagle text orientate the reader to what is coming in the subsequent paragraph(s) but there is also the first sentence that typically adds to that function. It is not only the location of hyper-themes that matters, it is also their content. For example, headings and sub-headings are typically nominalisations that 'summarise' the content of the paragraph. Yet, if we deleted the sub-headings, the reader should still be able to predict what the paragraph will be about by reading the remaining phases of the hyper-themes. For example, if we look at the first lines of each paragraph, we can identify the following:

- in the classification, the technical name is stated and 'family' is used
- in the appearance phase, we have 'has an appearance'
- in the diet phase, 'diet' and 'hunts for its food' are chosen
- in the breeding phase, the terms 'pair for life' and 'nest' are chosen to signify the two paragraphs' functions, respectively
- in the threats phase, there is the use of 'threatens'.

We could read further into all of the first sentences but for three of them (the two in 'Diet' and the one in 'Threats'), it is sufficient for the reader to read the shaded parts to be prepared for what is coming in each paragraph.

THE SEA EAGLE

Classification

The Sea Eagle (Haliaeetus albicilla) is a large bird of prey in the Accipitradae family. It is found all year round in an area covering large parts of northern Europe and northern Asia, as well as coastal areas of the continents in the Southern Hemisphere.

Appearance

The Sea Eagle has an appearance that makes it stand out. Overall, it is very large with a wingspan of around 2.5 metres and a length up to a metre. Its head is large and both its talons (claws) and beak are large and very powerful. The male, as in most birds of prey, is smaller than the female, with the female weighing up to 7 kg. ...

Diet

The Sea Eagle's diet is diverse and consists mainly of a range of seafood; for example, relatively small fish such as trout and large fish such as salmon. Just about any fish that is found near the water's surface is potential prey. The Sea Eagle also feeds on other sea birds; small mammals such as mice and rabbits; and carrion.

The Sea Eagle hunts for its food either by searching an area by gliding over it or by taking up a strategic position at a high point on land to scout the surroundings. Depending on the size of the prey, it is eaten by the Sea Eagle where it is caught or nearby, or it is carried in the bird's talons to the nest.

Breeding

Sea Eagles pair for life once a bond is formed after their territory has been established. A pair produces only one to three eggs per year, usually in early Spring. Both parents take care of the eggs over the 38 days before they hatch. The female is typically in charge of the brooding and feeding the chicks. It takes more than six months for the chicks to develop to the stage where they can be independent.

The Sea Eagle's nest is very large and remarkably heavy, about 500 kg. It is constructed with plant materials, such as large branches for the base and softer grasses and moss for the interior. The same nests are added to for many, many years, even by generations of Sea Eagles, and so can grow up to two metres in diameter. To allow for hunting and the safety of the chicks and to accommodate the size of these nests, they are typically located at the top of huge, well established trees or on the ledges of coastal cliffs.

Threats

Anything that threatens their nests and, hence, their chicks, or diminishes their food supply threatens the existence of the Sea Eagle. Therefore, logging, accumulated toxins in their prey because of pollution, hunting, egg stealing, intentional poisoning and even the blades of wind turbines can all pose major or minor threats to the Sea Eagle.

Figure 48: Orientations in a Description at paragraph level

Orientations in the non-temporal explaining, and the arguing genres

Hyper-themes and macro-themes play an important role in Factorial and Consequential Explanations as well as Arguments and Discussions. All of these genres generally use hyper- and macro-themes in similar ways. The text in Figure 49 shows how the first paragraph acts as macro-theme, preparing the reader for what they will find in the text. There are phases within this stage of the text: the first line tells the reader what the field is and its significance in the world, then it defines the topic and then it lists the four aspects of the problem to be covered. We would expect that the number of aspects is the number addressed in the text, and the order of the aspects is the order we would meet them in the rest of the text. With each aspect being coloured, it is clear that the paragraphs come in the same order as given in the macro-theme, which is boxed in Fig. 49 and 50. Each aspect is simply mentioned in the macro-theme so it is the function of the hyper-theme to elaborate on the aspect a little more. However, the hyper-themes do not need a lot of detail because their purpose is to predict for the reader what the paragraph will handle. It is the function of the remainder of the paragraph to expand and elaborate on the hyper-themes by providing new information. If we take up the notion of given and new information, we can see that, once the aspects of the text are presented in the macro-theme and, as newest information within the macro-theme they come last, the hyper-themes can be seen as presenting mainly given information.

WHAT ARE THE CONSEQUENCES OF AIR POLLUTION IN HONG KONG?

Air pollution is increasingly a major problem for cities around the globe, including Shanghai, Beijing and Hong Kong. Air pollution can be defined as the presence of airborne particles that are harmful to the well-being of animal and plant life. The quality of life in Hong Kong is negatively affected by air pollution in several ways and they include: rising temperatures, degradation of visibility, acid rain and depletion of the ozone layer.

Rising temperatures are the major result of the greenhouse effect, which, in turn, lead to droughts and increasing sea levels. The greenhouse effect is the name given to the atmosphere behaving in the same way as a greenhouse, which allows certain radiation to enter the glasshouse but stops other radiation escaping. More precisely, objects on the earth absorb UV light and emit low-energy infra-red radiation, which is trapped by the earth's atmosphere, resulting in increased temperatures. The effect is worsened when the atmosphere is concentrated with air particles and/or pollutants such as water vapour, carbon monoxide, carbon dioxide and methane. Hong Kong will be greatly affected by at least one of the suggested consequences of increased global temperatures and that is the rise in sea level caused by the melting polar regions. With much of Hong Kong hugging the coastline, any rise in the sea level would be disastrous for urban areas and food supplies as fish populations and farming areas are adversely affected. Also, the impact of hotter and extended summers on the health of Hong Kong's elderly citizens will be an increasing concern.

Visibility degradation is caused by airborne particles, which scatter light and serve as condensation nuclei for clouds and fog. The particulates can come from natural phenomena such as volcanic eruptions, dust storms and sea spray or from human activities such as combustion. In Hong Kong, the combustion of fossil fuels in cars is the main contributor and the situation is worsened by the occurrence of photochemical smog, which is formed when smoke and exhaust fumes are trapped in a fog and undergo photochemical reactions.

Acid rain is a chemical phenomenon caused by the dissolution of nitrogen oxides and sulphur dioxide in rainwater to form nitric acid and sulphuric acid, respectively. The oxides are released during the combustion of fossil fuels by cars, factories and power plants. Acid rain has multiple adverse effects on ecosystems, where plants and soils are degraded, and on humans and property. Irritation of respiratory systems and corrosion of buildings and car bodies are some of the ways acid rain afflicts the people of Hong Kong.

The depletion of the ozone layer reduces the protection from harmful UV light that the ozone layer provides humans. The ozone layer is between 12km and 50km above the earth's surface and is being depleted by chlorofluorocarbons (CFCs), which react to break down the ozone. Although attempts have been made to replace CFCs, they are still widely used as solvents, refrigerants and aerosol propellants. Reducing the concentration of ozone will lead to greater amounts of UVB reaching the earth. This may cause problems such as skin cancers, eye disease and gene mutation.
In Hong Kong, air pollution is monitored by the Environmental Protection Department and its many initiatives have resulted in positive outcomes although further improvements can be made.

Figure 49: Macro-theme and hyper-themes in a Consequential Explanation

With the sample Discussion in Figure 50, arrows are used to indicate the magnitude of the orientations — the larger arrow to indicate that the macro-theme functions as orientation to the whole text, while the smaller arrows are for the hyper-themes. The meaning of the arrow looking back at the text is discussed shortly.

The macro-theme plays a significant role in this Discussion. That is not always the case but, in this example, it does. It even requires two paragraphs to achieve its function: to contextualise it historically and politically, but also to elaborate just slightly the aspects of expense, sustainability, cleanliness, and its high environmental and military risks. Then the two paragraphs in the arguments stage take up these aspects and balance the pros and cons. The hyper-theme for the first argument prepares the reader for a discussion about safety and cleanliness. The second hyper-theme signals the paragraph's content on cost and safety and we can see that this hyper-theme is made up of the first two sentences.

CAN NUCLEAR POWER HELP ANSWER OUR ENERGY NEEDS?

Nuclear power attracts diametrically opposed viewpoints: its advocates see it as relatively inexpensive and sustainable and a way to combat global warming, while its opponents see its waste as so toxic and long-lasting that it is a threat to the planet.

With respect to the emissions of greenhouse gases, nuclear power is a clean way of producing electricity when compared with coal-fired power stations, which meet most of the world's electricity demands. If the projections of the effect of global warming due to increased carbon dioxide emissions are correct, then nuclear energy is an antidote to consider carefully. Also, the fuel it uses, uranium, is more abundant than fossil fuels and much, much less is needed to produce the equivalent amount of energy.

Nevertheless, even though nuclear power stations produce fewer greenhouse gases than fossil-fuel power stations, they do present contamination risks to the planet with emissions of radioactivity and, more siginificantly, with the disposal of waste and accidents at the power plants. Nuclear waste requires very special treatment and storage methods so that the risks of the radioactive waste are minimised. However, despite all the planned precautions, human carelessness and natural disasters have caused very serious accidents at nuclear plants. For example, the explosion in the Chernobyl nuclear power plant in 1986 in the former USSR was due to human factors, while, more recently, in 2011, a human disaster was initiated by a natural disaster, a tsunami, at Fukushima in eastern Japan. The impact of both events have been catastrophic for their regions and will continue to be for a very long time.

Many major accidents have also happened in the mining of fossil fuels and in the production of power from those fuels. It is the case that many more people have died from the negative consequences of fossil fuels than from nuclear power (New Scientist 2011). So why are people so fearful of nuclear energy? Perhaps it is the fact that deaths from fossil fuels occur in smaller numbers over a long time soan whereas nuclear accidents tend to be catastrophic. Also, the high level of toxicity of the by-products of nuclear energy length and the time they remain toxic makes many think it is too great a risk to take. In order to make nuclear power and the storage of the waste material safer, expensive research and development is needed. This cost would be too great for many developing countries where capital and technology are limited. But even in affluent, developed countries, safety is still a major concern, as the Fukushima catastrophe shows.

Nuclear power seems to have various advantages. It is relatively sustainable, efficient, clean and inexpensive. However, at the same time, the waste issues still hinder its development as a major and common source of power. Fossil fuels that currently fire the majority of the power plants are not a viable long-term option either due to global warming. In the long run, therefore, it seems that renewable alternatives to the use of both radioactive fuels and fossil fuels offer solutions to future power needs.

Figure 50: Macro-theme and hyper-theme patterns in a Discussion

The big difference between the arguing genres and the explaining genres is that the Arguments and Discussions end with what Martin (1992: 454) calls macro-new. In Figure 50, the arrow pointing back up to the text represents the purpose of the macro-new as re-orientating the reader to the accumulated meanings in the text. It assumes the reader has read the text and it typically gives a recommendation, even if it is couched in uncertainty. The content of the macro-new is a result of the accumulated new meanings given in the body of the text, typically towards the end of the paragraphs as the new meanings 'pile up'.

Language patterns for expressing uncertainty and including other perspectives

> "Recognition of uncertainty is a characteristic of the scientific method…"
> Tim Palmer[1]

The above quote asserts that uncertainty is a central feature of the scientific method but often little attention is paid to the language resources for expressing the appropriate degree of uncertainty. Uncertainty can be found in all scientific texts of all the range of genres in science. In the discussion and conclusion stages of Laboratory Reports, those students who show control of the language of uncertainty are often identified, explicitly or implicitly, as having a deeper understanding.

Language resources for expressing uncertainty

Uncertainty can be seen as any degree between the extremes of 'It is' and 'It is not'. Figure 51 presents a range of language resources for expressing varying degrees of uncertainty or possibility (Halliday & Matthiessen 2014) and these are typically included as components of modality. Modal resources are some of the functional groupings that realise the tenor of a context. Whereas the groupings for realising the field were brick-like, where we had 'bricks' of processes, participants and circumstances, and the groupings for realising the mode were wave-like, where we talked about the flow of a text through the orientations expressed through choices in theme-rheme and given-new, the groupings for realising tenor are more wash-like. Like a watercolour that has seepage or a merging of colours, the language resources realising the interpersonal meanings can be spread throughout the clause and the whole text, in the grammar and in the lexis, too. But, it is not only in the grammar and lexis. In speech, we have the phonological choices as well. These

---

1. Accessed 21 Apr 2013 from http://royalsociety.org/further/uncertainty-in-science/

choices cover the ways words and clauses are said aloud, for example, through intonation and stress.

Our focus in this book is on the resources that deal with the exchange of information in science classrooms and that is why we are focusing on the choices that are concerned with degrees of possibility (degrees of uncertainty) and degrees of frequency. As we will see in the texts that follow, there are many resources (Fig. 51) available when working with the language for interacting. The resources listed are organised from what is typically chosen in spoken contexts at the top (could, may) to what is typically chosen in written texts (probability, risk). Expressing opinions, or including various perspectives, can be seen as a grammatically metaphorical way of expressing uncertainty. For example, 'They claim that neutrinos travel faster than the speed of light' can be seen as a metaphorical way of expressing 'Neutrinos may travel faster than the speed of light'.

Degrees of certainty	**Examples**
could, might, may, will, must,	The cancer could be benign.
perhaps, maybe, possibly, probably, certainly, surely	The cancer is probably benign.
They think, Scientists believe, Scientists claim, Research suggests that, It suggests that ...,	I think that the cancer is benign. The results suggest that the cancer is benign.
impossible, uncertain, possible, likely, positive, certain, ...	It is possible that the cancer is benign.
According to..., Apparently, In my opinion, ...	According to the results, the cancer is benign.
possibility, certainty, probability, risk, chance, likelihood	There is a 30% risk that it is prostate cancer.
Degrees of frequency	
rarely, sometimes, usually, generally, always, ...	Colorectal cancers usually begin as benign polyps.
rare, unusual, common, usual, frequent, ...	Skin cancer is the most common cancer in the U.S.A.
frequency, tendency, ...	There is a tendency for some cancers to be inherited.

Figure 51: Some common language resources for expressing uncertainty.

Within each modal resource, it is possible to organise the choices along a cline (Fig. 52) of definiteness so that 'it may be' is less definite than 'it will be', which is less definite than 'it must be'. For example, it would be acceptable to say that 'It has to be oxygen' or 'It must be oxygen' is higher certainty than 'It might be oxygen'. Of course, in any context, there can always be attempts, be they successful or unsuccessful, to subvert these meanings but the kinds of texts and classroom contexts we are concerned with, we can say that Figure 52 presents the typical gradations of modal resources.

low	median	high
could, might, may	should, ought to	will, must
perhaps, maybe, possibly	probably, generally	certainly
They think that..., They feel that..., It seems that...	It suggests that..., They believe that...	They claim that..., They know that...
possible	likely, probable	positive, sure, certain
never, rarely, seldom, occasionally	generally, frequently, often, regularly	usually, always
rare, occasional, infrequent	general, frequent	regular, usual

Figure 52: Modal resources organised according to a cline of definiteness

The nominalised forms (probability, risk, chance and frequency) have not been included in the table because we cannot say that one is higher in certainty than another since each of these can be quantified and qualified in some way. For example, it is possible to say a 10% chance, or a 60% risk, or a probability of 99%.

Text 57a identifies the modal resources (bold italics) we have covered. As an example of a Description, it attempts to present the information known about pesticides in a balanced way so that a neutral tenor is established.

Text 57a

PESTICIDES

Pesticides and cancer

Pesticides are ***widely*** used in agriculture and have been linked to various types of cancers, including breast cancer, bowel cancer, leukaemia, and lymphomas. Although high doses of ***some*** of these chemicals ***can*** cause cancer in animals, the effects on humans have been ***inconclusive***.

Pesticides on fruit and vegetables

Fruit and vegetables ***sometimes*** contain very small amounts of pesticides. Because of this, it is recommended that fruit and vegetables are rinsed before eating. But there is no ***evidence*** that these small amounts ***can*** increase cancer ***risk***. ***In fact***, eating lots of fruit and vegetables ***can*** reduce your ***risk*** of several cancers, despite pesticide residues on them.

Pesticides in the environment

Some potentially dangerous pesticides such as DDT and Lindane are now banned worldwide for agricultural use. Because these chemicals break down slowly, they ***can*** accumulate in the environment and so ***eventually*** find their way up the food chain and be stored in our fatty tissues. Even so, scientists across different research groups and countries have ***consistently found*** that there is not a ***definitive*** link between these chemicals and cancer.

There could be discussion about any of the choices in the text and people's readings of them could vary greatly. For example, 'inconclusive' could easily be argued. Including references to the data and research on pesticides might help but it is the nature of science to promote discussion and further testing. Having 'very small', which has not been bolded here, rather than the specific measurement of the pesticide might be picked up and argued about by a reader. It could be said by someone who was against any pesticide use that choosing 'very small' glides over the importance of even small amounts of pesticides in fruit and vegetables for babies.

For students, the significance of developing control of the modal resources is that, when they read about science or view and listen to people talk about science, they are more equipped to understand how definite that knowledge is being constructed and how it can be questioned. But also when they discuss and write their own scientific meanings, such as in the discussion and conclusion stages of Laboratory Reports and Investigations, they need to be able to show that they have a deeper understanding of the science through using these modal resources appropriately. The irony is that 'the more you know, the more you know you don't know.' The two extracts that follow illustrate modal choices (major ones in bold) made by two students in their writing.

Extract from a Laboratory Report

Different respiratory substrates have different effects on the rate of respiration of yeast cells. ***It appears*** *that the 1% sucrose solution shows the greatest rate of respiration of yeast cells, while the 1% starch solution shows the slowest. The respiratory rate of the 1% starch solution is* ***approximately*** *the same as that of distilled water.*

Extract from an Investigation

While speaking Swedish to my plant did not make ***much of*** *a difference in growth, the plant that I spoke to* ***did appear*** *healthier but* ***I can't say*** *that my* ***prediction*** *was accurate without further tests.*

I felt *my measuring was* ***relatively*** *accurate. However, the time constraints imposed meant that error due to rushing was* ***possible****.*

Perhaps *ensuring that the amount of Swedish spoken was* ***exactly*** *the same each time* ***could*** *also help.*

If *I was to do the experiment again,* ***I would like*** *to be able to go and see the plants* ***more often*** *and grow more than two to improve the* ***credibility*** *of the results.*

We could consider what these extracts would read like without the modality: there wouldn't be any room for human error, no optional choices, no alternative viewpoints, nor any ways of considering improvements to the experiment design.

Including other perspectives

The examples in Figures 51 and 52 that deal with mental processes (think, feel, believe) and saying processes (say, claim, state, assert), and elements such as 'in my opinion' can be seen as explicit ways for other perspectives to be included in the text. For example:

> ***Farmers report*** *that salespeople had, for years, been visiting farms in dairy areas hawking "protein powder" additives, which would often be delivered in unmarked brown paper bags of 25 kg each.*

> ***Scientists across different research groups and countries have consistently found*** *that there is not a definitive link between these chemicals and cancer.*

With 'farmers report' and 'scientists found', we can point to the general group that holds the opinion and either agree with them or argue against them. However, it is still not clear who specifically holds that opinion and we would need to know the names of the farmers and the names of the scientists or science research groups.

In this next example, it is difficult to know where to start looking unless it is explicitly stated somewhere else in the text which specific research is being referred to:

> ***Research shows*** *that there is no definitive link between these chemicals and cancer.*

The resources for expressing perspectives can be located on the register continuum, according to how spoken or written they are. In the following, the list begins with the typically more spoken and ends with the typically more written: I believe, we believe, they believe, scientists believe, the research shows, it is claimed, the claim. We can see that the pattern in the orientations for each is to move from the individual to groups of more expert people to their work and data until we end up with the most abstract.

This kind of critical understanding is important for students when searching for information, be it on the internet or in textbooks, or when engaging in any number of texts about science that are produced by mass media or being promoted by special interest groups.

Returning to Text 57a, we can ask whether there are other questions that could be asked of the interpersonal meanings in the text, not just those that were identified in bold italics. In

Text 57b, the highlighted elements with possible questions in brackets identify the kind of interrogation of the meanings in a text that teachers and students ought to be able to carry out.

Text 57b

PESTICIDES

Pesticides and cancer

Pesticides are widely used in agriculture and ***have been linked*** *(Who has linked them?)* to various types of cancers, including breast cancer, bowel cancer, leukaemia, and lymphomas. Although high doses of some of these chemicals can cause cancer in animals, the effects on humans have been ***inconclusive***. *(How inconclusive? What was the methodology?)*

Pesticides on fruit and vegetables

Fruit and vegetables sometimes contain ***very small amounts*** *(What specifically are these amounts and how do we know they are safe?)* of pesticides. Because of this, ***it is recommended*** *(Who is recommending?)* that fruit and vegetables are rinsed before eating. But there ***is no evidence*** *(What was the methodology?)* that these small amounts can increase cancer risk. In fact, eating lots of fruit and vegetables can reduce your risk of several cancers, despite pesticide residues on them.

Pesticides in the environment

Some potentially dangerous pesticides such as DDT and Lindane ***are now banned*** *(Who has banned them and who has not?)* worldwide for agricultural use. Because these chemicals break down slowly, they can accumulate in the environment and so eventually find their way up the food chain and be stored in our fatty tissues. Even so, ***scientists across different research groups and countries have consistently found*** *(Which scientists and research groups and which countries and how consistently and what was their methodology?)* that there ***is not a definitive*** *(Again, what was the methodology?)* link between these chemicals and cancer.

Classroom activities for developing modal resources

How could teachers and students work with this understanding in the classroom? Since modality, as focused on in this book, is about the various degrees of something being certain or not, then the focus for the classroom activities should be about placing the students in contexts, such as an experiment, where it is not possible to be sure about what they are observing, or not sure of the causes of the effects they are observing.

Other activities could get them to work with written texts and change the degree or kind of modality in some way. The next two sample activities are illustrations of this approach.

Sample activity 1

Text 57c is an example in which the modal resources have been deleted from the text as much as possible.

Text 57c

PESTICIDES

Pesticides and cancer

Pesticides are used in agriculture and have been linked to various types of cancers, including breast cancer, bowel cancer, leukaemia, and lymphomas. High doses of these chemicals cause cancer in animals and humans.

Pesticides on fruit and vegetables

Fruit and vegetables contain very small amounts of pesticides. Because of this, fruit and vegetables are rinsed before eating because these small amounts increase cancer. Eating lots of fruit and vegetables reduces several cancers, despite pesticide residues on them.

Pesticides in the environment

Dangerous pesticides such as DDT and Lindane are now banned worldwide for agricultural use. Because these chemicals break down slowly, they accumulate in the environment and so find their way up the food chain and are stored in our fatty tissues. Even so, scientists across different research groups and countries have found that there is not a link between these chemicals and cancer.

Even though it is difficult to take out all the modal resources, it is clear how 'strange' the modified text reads and, therefore, how dependent and how normal it is to use modal resources, even though, as readers, we are often not aware of their use.

Sample activity 2

Another classroom activity is to add modal resources where there weren't any, and another is to modulate the existing modal resources by increasing or decreasing their intensity. These activities are illustrated in Text 58, which is made up of three versions of an extract from a text on colour blindness.

Text 58[2]

COLOUR BLINDNESS

Low degree of certainty

Colour blindness may be a hereditary condition or may be caused by disease of the optic nerve or retina. Acquired colour vision problems may affect the eye with the disease and may become progressively worse over time. Patients with a colour vision defect caused by disease sometimes have trouble discriminating blues and yellows. Inherited colour blindness is fairly common, affecting both eyes and not worsening over time. This type is found in about 8% of males and 0.4% of females. These colour problems might be linked to the X chromosome and could be passed from a mother to her son.

Median degree of certainty

Colour blindness is probably a hereditary condition or caused by disease of the optic nerve or retina. Acquired colour vision problems generally only affect the eye with the disease and typically become progressively worse over time. Patients with a colour vision defect caused by disease usually have trouble discriminating blues and yellows. Inherited colour blindness is generally the most common, affecting both eyes and not worsening over time. This type is found in about 8% of males and 0.4% of females. These colour problems are often linked to the X chromosome and most of the time are passed from a mother to her son.

High degree of certainty

Colour blindness is either a hereditary condition or caused by disease of the optic nerve or retina. Acquired colour vision problems only affect the eye with the disease and usually become progressively worse over time. Patients with a colour vision defect caused by disease almost always have trouble discriminating blues and yellows. Inherited colour blindness is the most common, affecting both eyes and not worsening over time. This type is found in about 8% of males and 0.4% of females. These colour problems are linked to the X chromosome and are invariably passed from a mother to her son.

2. Adapted from http://www.fightingblindness.ie/colour-blindness/. Accessed 21 Dec 2015.

References

Callaghan, M. and Rothery, J. (1988) **Teaching Factual Writing: A Genre-Based Approach**. Sydney: Metropolitan East Disadvantaged Schools Program.

Christie, F. (1997) 'Curriculum macrogenres as forms of initiation into a culture'. In Christie, F. and Martin, J.R. (eds) (1997) **Genre and Institutions: Social Processes in the Workplace and School**. London: Continuum.

Christie, F. (1998) 'Science and apprenticeship: the pedagogic discourse'. In Martin, J.R. and Veel, R. (eds) **Reading Science: Critical and Functional Perspectives on Discourses of Science**. London: Routledge.

Christie, F. (2002) **Classroom Discourse Analysis: A Functional Perspective**. London, Continuum.

Christie, F. and Derewianka, B. (2008) **School Discourse: Learning to Write Across the Years of Schooling**. London: Continuum.

Christie, F. and Martin, J.R. (eds) (1997) **Genre and Institutions: Social Processes in the Workplace and School**. London: Continuum.

Custance, B., Dare, B. and Polias, J. (2011) **How Language Works: Success in Literacy and Learning**. Adelaide: Department of Education and Child Development (South Australia).

Dansie, B. (2001) 'Scaffolding oral language: "The Hungry Giant" retold'. In Hammond, J. (ed.) **Scaffolding: Teaching and Learning in Language and Literacy Education**. Newtown, NSW: Primary English Teaching Association.

EDB (2009) **Integrated Science Curriculum & Assessment Guide (Secondary 4-6)** http://www.edb.gov.hk/attachment/en/curriculum-development/kla/science-edu/int_sci_final_e_20091005.pdf [accessed 4 April 2013]

Forey, G. and Polias, J. (forthcoming) 'Multi-semiotic resources providing maximal input in teaching science through English'. In Llinares, A. and Morton, T. (eds) **Applied Linguistics Perspectives on CLIL**. Amsterdam: Benjamins.

Halliday, M.A.K. (1975) **Learning How to Mean: Explorations in the Development of Language**. London: Edward Arnold.

Halliday, M.A.K. (1985) **Spoken and Written Language**. Geelong, Victoria: Deakin University Press.

Halliday, M.A.K. (1993) 'General orientation'. In Halliday, M.A.K. and Martin, J.R. **Writing Science: Literacy and Discursive Power**. London: Falmer Press.

Halliday, M.A.K. (2003) 'On the "architecture" of human language'. In **On Language and Linguistics**. Volume 3 in the Collected Works of M.A.K. Halliday. London and New York: Equinox. p.27.

Halliday, M.A.K. and Matthiessen, C.M.I.M. (4th ed.) (2014) **Halliday's Introduction to Functional Grammar**. London: Routledge.

Hammond, J. (2001) 'Scaffolding and language'. In Hammond, J. (ed.) **Scaffolding: Teaching and Learning in Language and Literacy Education**. Newtown, NSW: Primary English Teaching Association.

Hedeboe, J. and Polias, J. (2008) **Genrebyrån: En Språkpedagogisk Funktionell Grammatik i Kontext**. Stockholm: Hallgren and Fallgren.

Iedema, R., Feez, S., and White, P.R.R. (1994) **Media Literacy**. Sydney: Disadvantaged Schools Program, NSW Department of School Education.

Lemke, J. (1998) 'Multiplying meaning: visual and verbal semiotics in scientific text'. In Martin, J.R. and Veel, R. (eds) **Reading Science: Critical and Functional Perspectives on Discourses of Science**. London: Routledge.

Martin, J.R. (1992) **English Text: System and Structure**. Amsterdam: John Benjamins.

Martin, J.R. (1995) 'Text and clause: fractal resonance'. **Text**. 15.1: 5–42.

Martin, J.R. (1999) 'Mentoring semogenesis: genre-based literacy pedagogy.' In Christie, F. (ed.) **Pedagogy and the Shaping of Consciousness: Linguistic and Social Processes**. London: Cassell.

Martin, J.R. (2012) 'Language in education'. In Wang Z. (ed.) **Collected Works of J.R. Martin**. Vol.7. Shanghai: Shanghai Jiao Tong University Press.

Martin, J.R. and Rose, D. (2nd ed.) (2007) **Working with Discourse: Meaning Beyond the Clause**. London: Bloomsbury.

Martin, J.R. and Rose, D. (2008) **Genre Relations: Mapping Culture**. London: Equinox.

Matthiessen, C.M.I.M. (1993) 'Register in the round: diversity in a unified theory of register analysis'. In Ghadessy, M. (ed.) **Register Analysis: Theory and Practice**. London: Pinter.

Matthiessen, C.M.I.M. (2012) **Appliable Discourse Analysis** (in press).

Michell, M. and Sharpe, T. (2005) 'Collective instructional scaffolding in English as a second language classrooms.' **Prospect** 20(1) April, 31-58.

Painter, C. (1996) 'The development of language as a resource for thinking: a linguistic view of learning'. In Hasan, R. and Williams, G. (eds) **Literacy in Society**. London: Longman.

Polias, J. (2003) **ESL Scope and Scales**. South Australia: Department of Education and Children's Services. (Accessed at <http://www.lexised.com/writing/>)

Polias, J. (ed.) (2005) **Improving Language and Learning in Public-sector Schools**. Hong Kong: Education and Manpower Bureau.

Polias, J. (2006) **Lesson Observation Report 2006**. (Accessed at <http://www.lexised.com/resources/>)

Polias, J. (2007a) **Lesson Observation Report for ILLIPS 2007**. (Accessed at <http://www.lexised.com/resources/>)

Polias, J. (ed.) (2007b) **BLMCSS Mentoring 2006-2007**. (Accessed at <http://www.lexised.com/resources/>

Polias, J. (2008a) 'A teaching scope and sequence for successful learning'. Keynote at the conference: **The Missing LINC? Understanding the Role of Language in Learning Across the Curriculum**. Aston University, Birmingham, UK, 8 November 2008.

Polias, J. (ed.) (2008b) **SKHTSKSS Mentoring 2007-2008**. (Accessed at <http://www.lexised.com/resources/>

Polias, J. (2010) 'Pedagogical resonance: improving teaching and learning'. In Coffin, C. (ed.) "Systemic Functional Linguistics", Special edition of the **National Association for Language Development in the Curriculum (NALDIC) Quarterly,** Autumn 8(1), United Kingdom.

Polias, J. and Forey, G. (2016) 'Teaching through English: maximal input in meaning making'. In Bayley, P. and Miller, D.R. (eds) **On Permeable Contexts and Hybrid Discourses: Preliminaries**. London: Equinox.

Rothery, J. (1996) 'Making changes: developing an educational linguistics'. In Hasan, R. and Williams, G. (eds) **Literacy in Society**. London: Longman.

Sharpe, T. (2001) 'Scaffolding in action: snapshots from the classroom'. In Hammond, J. (ed.) **Scaffolding: Teaching and Learning in Language and Literacy Education**. Newtown, NSW: Primary English Teaching Association.

Unsworth, L. (2001) 'Evaluating the language of different types of explanations in junior high school science texts.' **International Journal of Science Education** 23(6), 585-609.

van Lier, L. (2004) **The ecology and semiotics of language learning**. Dordrecht: Kluwer Academic.

Veel, R. (1997) 'Learning how to mean — scientifically speaking: apprenticeship into scientific discourse in the secondary school.' In Christie, F. and Martin, J.R. (eds) **Genre and Institutions: Social Processes in the Workplace and School**. London: Continuum.

Vygotsky, L. (1963) **Thought and Language**. Cambridge, MA: MIT Press.

Wood, D., Bruner, J.S. and Ross, G. (1976) 'The role of tutoring in problem solving'. **Journal of Child Psychology & Psychiatry and Allied Disciplines**. 17, 89-100

Index

A

abstraction 71, 72, 113, 124, 138, 140
active voice 110, 148, 149
Argument 12, 43, 44, 45, 46, 47, 153, 155, 157

B

Biography 12, 48, 49, 65, 66

C

causal relations 131, 132
cause and effect 33, 131, 139
certainty 46, 71, 158, 159, 160, 166 *(also uncertainty)*
circumstances 37, 109, 110, 113, 115, 121, 125, 158
classification 24, 25, 64, 151, 152
Classification 12, 26, 31, 72, 118, 129
classifier 116, 117, 119, 120
cohesion 129
Comparison 12, 26, 28
complex 116
Component 12, 14, 26, 30, 31, 58, 141, 148
Consequential Explanation 12, 33, 38, 40, 42, 52, 53, 119, 127, 153, 154
contingent 82, 83, 88, 98
cycle of teaching and learning 5, 8, 97, 101, 102, 103, 104, 105 *(also teaching and learning cycle)*

D

definitions 25, 120, 122
describer 116, 117, 119, 120, 140
Description 12, 24, 25, 26, 27, 51, 52, 64, 150, 151, 152, 160
Discussion 12, 43, 44, 45, 46, 153, 155, 156, 157
do-er 111, 125, 149, 150
done-to 111, 149

E

Experiment 12, 18, 19, 23, 72, 77, 78, 79, 109, 110, 111, 112
Explanations 12, 33, 34, 36, 38, 42, 45, 72

F

Factorial Explanations 12, 33, 38, 39, 42, 153
field 70, 71, 72, 73, 74, 86, 90, 92, 93, 94 105, 108
frequency 126, 159
functional model of language 9, 69, 70, 74, 107, 110 *(also systemic-functional model of language)*

G

generic structure 19, 22, 136
genre(s) 10, 11, 12, 13, 14, 17, 24, 25, 33, 35, 38, 43, 45, 48, 51, 52, 60, 63, 64, 69, 70, 72, 77, 79, 80, 82, 95, 97, 101, 103, 105, 109, 111, 112, 129, 136, 141, 150, 153, 157, 158
given 142, 144, 146, 147, 153, 158
guided construction 101, 102, 104 *(also joint construction)*

H

hyper-theme 150, 151, 153, 154, 155, 156

I

independent construction 101, 102, 104, 135
Investigations 12, 22, 23, 110, 161, 162

L

Laboratory Report 11, 12, 20, 22, 23, 72, 80, 81, 103, 104, 105, 110, 123, 158, 161, 162
lexical items 113, 114, 125, 129, 130, 150
lexical cohesion 129
lexical complexity 125 *(also lexical simplicity)*
lexical relations 129, 130
lexis 77, 78, 79, 94, 158

M

macrogenre 14, 33, 45, 51, 52, 58, 123
macro-new 157

macro-scaffold 77, 79, 80, 81, 82, 103, 107, 109, 111, 112
macro-scaffolding 8, 72, 77, 82, 83, 138
macro-theme 150, 151, 153, 154, 155, 156
meso-scaffolding 8, 72, 77, 82, 83, 88, 95, 102, 128
micro-scaffolding 8, 77, 82, 83, 98, 99, 101, 102, 103, 128
modality 158, 162, 165
modal resources 158, 160, 161, 165, 166
mode 70, 71, 72, 73, 74, 90, 92, 93, 94 108, 137, 158
modelling and deconstruction 97, 101, 102, 104, 105, 133, 134
multisemiotic 7, 57, 96

N

new 27, 37, 46, 49, 136, 142, 144, 146, 147, 153, 157, 158
nominal group 109, 114, 115, 116, 117, 118, 119, 120, 121, 122, 125, 138, 139, 140
nominalisation 123, 124, 125, 126, 127, 128, 138, 139, 148, 151
numerative 116, 117, 118, 119

O

orientation 19, 23, 27, 37, 49, 66, 80, 108, 110, 111, 136, 137, 138, 139, 140, 142, 147, 148, 149, 150, 152, 153, 155, 158, 163

P

participant 109, 110, 111, 113, 115, 121, 122, 125, 149, 158
passive voice 79, 110, 111, 148, 149, 150
pedagogical resonance 8, 58, 63, 64, 105
pointer 116, 117, 118, 119
Procedural Recount 79, 80, 110, 111, 112, 138
process 37, 109, 110, 111, 113, 121, 125, 126, 129, 132, 136, 137, 147, 149, 163
Protocol 12, 19

Q

qualifier 116, 118, 119, 120, 122, 140

R

register 70, 71, 72, 73, 74, 77, 79, 80, 81, 82, 83, 84, 85, 87, 89, 95, 96, 107, 108, 111, 112, 123, 124, 125, 163
register continuum 72, 73, 77, 81, 82, 83, 85, 87, 89, 95, 96, 108, 111, 123, 124, 125, 163
rheme 136, 142, 158

S

scaffolding 8, 11, 54, 63, 77, 82, 83, 85, 91, 96, 97, 98, 99, 102, 105, 108, 124, 128, 135, 144 (*also scaffold*)
semiotic 7, 8, 11, 13, 71
Sequential Explanation 12, 33, 34, 35, 36, 37, 42, 51, 52, 53, 58, 59, 65, 72, 79, 80, 81, 111, 112, 113, 118, 133, 134, 135, 136, 141, 144, 145, 146, 147, 148
setting the context 101, 102, 104
signposting 60, 61

T

technicality 36, 71, 113, 124, 138, 140, 148
tenor 70, 71, 72, 73, 74, 90, 92, 93, 94, 108, 137, 158, 160
theme 136, 137, 140, 141, 142, 148, 150, 151, 158
Theoretical Explanations 12, 33, 38, 41, 42
thing 116, 117, 118, 119, 120, 122, 123, 140

CPSIA information can be obtained
at www.ICGtesting.com
Printed in the USA
BVXC01n1545221216
5022BVAU00004B/8

* 9 7 8 0 6 4 6 9 5 2 6 0 4 *